Z.

THE POETRY TRIALS

CREATIVE VOICES

Edited by Donna Samworth

First published in Great Britain in 2016 by:
YoungWriters
Remus House
Coltsfoot Drive
Peterborough
PE2 9BF
Telephone: 01733 890066
Website: www.youngwriters.co.uk

Book Design by Ashley Janson

SB ISBN 978-1-78624-197-9
Printed and bound in the UK by BookPrintingUK
Website: www.bookprintinguk.com

FOREWORD

Welcome, Reader!

For Young Writers' latest competition, *The Poetry Trials*, we gave secondary school students nationwide the challenge of writing a poem. They were given the option of choosing a restrictive poetic technique, or to choose any poetic style of their choice. They rose to the challenge magnificently, with young writers up and down the country displaying their poetic flair.

We chose poems for publication based on style, expression, imagination and technical skill. The result is this entertaining collection full of diverse and imaginative poetry, which is also a delightful keepsake to look back on in years to come.

Here at Young Writers our aim is to encourage creativity in the next generation and to inspire a love of the written word, so it's great to get such an amazing response, with some absolutely fantastic poems. It made choosing the winners extremely difficult, so well done to *Amy Berton* who has been chosen as the best in this book. Their poem will go into a shortlist from which the top 5 poets will be selected to compete for the ultimate Poetry Trials prize.

I'd like to congratulate all the young poets in *The Poetry Trials - Creative Voices* - I hope this inspires them to continue with their creative writing.

Editorial Manager

A POEM IS JUST THE BEGINNING...

CONTENTS

THE POEMS

ETERNITY

On an empty path,
I walk alone,
In a colourless world,
Of the unknown.

Like the perpetual sea waves,
Reaching for the shore,
Like a long-forgotten path,
Living alone from the lore.

Every day, rises the sun,
But the brilliant rays,
Always fail to illuminate,
My indefinite dark days.

Ever wandering, ever searching,
On this unending journey,
For a steady destination,
Which constantly eludes me.

And then you came,
Into my lonely life,
And saved my scarred soul,
From the endless strife.

Like an amazing summer breeze,
For the traveller weary,
On a parching hot day,
Like cool water of the vast sea.

The refreshing smell of seashore,
You carry with you,
Moments shared even if few,
I know now,
Happiness smells like you.

You are my reason to live again.

Adam William Torkoniak (14)

EXHALE YOUR YEARS

How tree branches shake as if they're coughing,
Clumps of dust recycled from vast overlooking skies,
Like a book possessed by times past,
Brought to life by uncontaminated hands.
Numbing taps of white,
Tainted drops scatter like eyelashes.
How a joyful landscape awakens,
While the world lays still,
Hills roll lazily under blank sheets in silence.
Why should this be a chore?
Wandering through tired, worn out streets,
Wading through everyday thoughts,
While the world is masked as such Arcadia.
I will anticipate my frosted breath,
As I think of memories passed,
Senseless,
And pull that book off from the shelf,
That is dead weight in your mind.
Flick through blank pages,
Which once functioned in thrilling technicolour,
Until you breathe in a dusty memory,
Buried and sensitive.
Nostalgia may furnish that cosy room,
Composed and edged with susurrus,
And bringing colours to your cheeks.
The shroudness of the morning mist,
That is what ageing means to me.

Niamh Stimpson (15)

SORRY

My hair scattered on the floor
Pride engraved with it.
Trust and love left behind
For the change to come.
I want to cover my eyes
But my hands are busy
Wiping the thunder shower
Cleansing my soul in my eyes.
Memories sneak out of my eyes
And roll down my eyes.
No way out and no way in.
An aching sensation runs
Through my sight to my heart.
It feels like I'm reaching for the stars,
You've kept it all under lock and key.
I've gone green with envy at the
Hands linked carelessly before me.
I haven't appreciated your words
Now I'm receiving silence.
I hear your silent scream
And is it too late to say sorry?

Qamar Said

ANXIETY

Its grip tightens,
It takes control of your heart,
Your will to survive diminishes, the moment the attack starts.

Reality disintegrates,
The blackness draws near,
It isn't the first nor the last time, and so you live in fear.

You try to fight,
But all your attempts are in vain,
The monster inside of you can never be slain.

It defeats you, throws you,
Into the darkest depths of your mind,
You aren't afraid of the darkness . . . you're afraid of what you'll find.

The silence deafening,
The emptiness fills you to the brim,
The panic calms you, in the certainty that you cannot win.

The loneliness is different,
Different from simply being alone,
The sadness all encompassing, as the monster reclaims the throne.

Isla Cartney (15)

DANCE MACABRE

The graveyard sleeps, all is still,
A raven caws, its call so shrill.

The dead sleep beneath the soil,
While their souls do endless toil.

The living are not welcome here;
They may not shed a tear.

For Satan rules this place.
To enter here, forsake your godly grace.

Gareth Thompson

LADY OF A SORT

Her eyes, I could stare into their reflection restlessly.
Her night-like pupils are perfectly complexioned with their moon-like lenses.
Blossomed summer roses fill her jowls
And I adore the dwell that invades her cheek time to time.
I like the shape that her mouth makes whenever she smiles.
I like the way it moves whenever she speaks.
The sound of her voice is nothing less than the sound of music.
But it's something easier to understand.
You could agree that she may be like the prayer people use for meditation,
For only she'll remain in one's thoughts like an internal dose of intoxication.

Bharatbir Singh Thind (13)

ANOTHER DAY IN THE LIFE

The place where footprints of the
heavy, sturdy boots lie, trodding, plodding, clodding.
Walking through the paper maker which once
used to be a deep milky bath,
a human weapon,
a nature reflector.

Beneath those waters the fortune of the workers stay.
As they walk down the alley that leads them to their fortune
in the cold winter's breeze,
all you hear is the scraping, shovelling,
the deafening noise of hollowing.

What scenes so far,
A war zone already.
This is where
The ghosts of the
Unknown workers belong.

Asha Hill (12)
Brannel School, St. Austell

THE OVER-SEEKER

I am just a lonely tree
Used to be free
Now this is me

Here I sit watching the workers picking away
Picking away

I'm slowly dying
Root by root
Branch by branch
The rot
Killing me over

Watching waste
Known as 'slurry'
Pumping through the industry

The noises loud and ringing
Through my thick, rough, splintering skin
The creatures whom used to burrow inside me
Gone to another place
Just to be safe

I'm alone
Where have my friends gone?
The small creatures
The other plants
Where are they?

The thick white material
Is more valuable than us, me
Why?
How?

The water builds up and slowly takes me
Far away
Every winter is unbearable

I see new schools ahead getting built
There, children happily going to school
Soon to see my happiness
But I still have it
Forever

Hope is all I need, and it's all I've got.

Alisha-May Lewis (12)
Brannel School, St. Austell

CHANGE IN SCHOOL

I started Year 7,
Lots of friends,
The boys,
The girls,
Everyone
Look at me now.

I started Year 8,
Everyone had changed,
Everyone wanted to be cool
Yet I was left behind.

I went to Year 9,
Teachers pushed the pressure,
I started to feel alone
Look at me now.

I am in Year 10,
Options are scary,
Exams are coming up,
Everything is different
I always hated change.

I will hate Year 11,
I don't want the change,
Even more pressure,
Exams are going to kill us
Please don't make me change.

Jordan Barkway (15)
Brannel School, St. Austell

THE WAR PIT

Chatter of a machine gun
Crack of a rifle
Screech of a pickaxe
Boom of a dynamite
Trenchfoot
Three feet deep, trench life
Gnawing hunger of starvation

Poverty, cold
My second skin peeling off in the bath
Cold sensation of beer
My empty wallet
My empty heart

Roar of the fire
Roar of the artillery
The laughing, the joking, the shouting
War, clay, pits
Much the same but oh so different

My body in France
My heart in Cornwall
A gun in my hands
Clay in my soul

A crack, a flash
A roar of guns
A scream, a shout
And searing pain

My body's broke
My throat is dry
My heart and soul in Cornwall
Digging in the war pit.

Sam Webber (13)
Brannel School, St. Austell

THE CLAY PITS

Each hit of the axe,
Triggers a new heartbeat.
Each dig of the earth,
Destroys my friends.

My friends are gone,
My heartbeat is increasing.
As plants disappear,
Workers are increasing.

My friends are the plants,
That grow when there is no work.
The green moss returns,
The hills become green again.

But as the sun turns the clay into dust,
I become older and weaker.
Every fire they light,
Burns me inside.

They are scarring me,
With every pit that they dig.
With every pile of clay,
Grows a new grey hair on my head.

But now the war has come,
My heart is slowing down.
My friends are returning,
But I am slowly dying.

Hyrum Willis (13)
Brannel School, St. Austell

DEPRESSION

Empty, desolate, abandoned
As the men of the tips go to war
Wives embracing their sadness and depression
With a small chance that they will come back
Killing their hearts with sorrow
Leaving them with searing pain

Children substituting their fathers
On the tips where the dead lay unknown
Lost ghosts wandering, trying to find the light,
Bodies covered by landslides made of the forbidden

No money being made
Leaving mothers and children to die of starvation
Children coming home from a long day at work
Coal staining their skin
Clay ruining their clothes
Costing more money to buy them out of life

Skin cut
Wounds infected
Coal poisoning their blood
Picking them off one by one
Lives ended
Depression filling
Life expectancy dropping
Plummeting our future.

Finlay Gallacher (13)
Brannel School, St. Austell

A FORGOTTEN TREASURE

Crunch, clatter, crash,
Blazing furnace, coal at heart
Deafening explosions emanate from the depths
Icy winds numb work-worn fingers
Crib, the only release from the white monotony;
Which engulfs them until the bell sounds freedom.
Until tomorrow.

Now, a war zone calling,
The relentless misery haunts the workers,
The abandonment of where their heart thrives;
Replaced with the pull of triggers and brutal deaths.
Sobbing descends from forlorn spouses,
Children oblivious to the fates ahead
An untouched beginning yet a fatal end.

Return in five years' time,
A mighty chasm, but,
Doomed ivy festoons droop like heavy tears,
Swirling dust rising to the bloodshot moon.
A foliage cascade shelters the forgotten contraption
The hoary waterwheel like a brain, a cog, thinking
A chaotic workplace, lost, gone.

Rebecca Odgers (12)
Brannel School, St. Austell

MY DAD

My dad
Bruises on his face
Blood oozing down his wrists
Trickling down his torso
Lounging in his pit

His ears the shape of cauliflowers
His eyes twisting when he stares
His stance wobbly
His heart burning flares

Day after day
Grows his insanity
And step by step
It kills his humanity

'The slurry pump, the skip'
He murmurs in his sleep
His sanity forgotten
Loitering like a creep.

Lewis Allely (12)
Brannel School, St. Austell

WHEAL MARTYN

Cracks that are filled with history,
Mossy walls abandoned and old,
Dimmed lights adding dimension to the walls.

Men's shoes stomping and the humming of their voices,
Their blistered hands trying to keep the ancestry going.

Outside is where they escape,
Rusted poles holding up the past.

The reflection in this stained device of light,
Tree sculpting the land.
A path leading towards the master's view.

Kiah Eve Truscott (12)
Brannel School, St. Austell

ANOTHER DAY . . .

Another man down,
Another day gone.
Another nightmare experienced,
Another night moved along

Another of his mates,
Passed away.
Another of his mates,
Ran astray.

Another day,
Another death,
Another dig,
Another breath.

Another dig,
Another boom.
Another man,
Will face his doom.

Max Burnett (13)
Brannel School, St. Austell

ERUPTION

When the water became foggy,
When the silver moon was at its peak,
When the once distant yelling became closer,
It was then they destroyed my land.

My once beautiful, peaceful haven,
Being torn, devoured, demolished,
An exploding volcano erupting
By the deranged creatures that call themselves men.

First they won, covering my world with cement and bricks.
Second we struck back, but slowly breaking what they made.
Third they took more of my creation, leaving us bare.
Last we did nothing, but we always come back, we're always here.

Aurora Burrowes (12)
Brannel School, St. Austell

MY MINING MAN

It was an accident the landslide,
The child's nightmare,
His heart pounding with adrenaline and fear,
Triggering every muscle,
His breath oozing from his mouth,
Breathless,
The soul seeker,
His fingertips blue and dusty,
His hands skulled red,
Blood streams down the mouth of a mining man,
White ghosts dragging from the 'dog hole',
The tapping,
The clay spills,
Crushing every worthless bone,
Now a sculpture of clay,
Moulded by the hands of the earth,
This was my mining man,
My mining man is to be no more.

Iceney Luke (12)
Brannel School, St. Austell

MY DAD

My dad's foot is rushing through the clay
Working harder than vehicles, day after day
My dad's eyes are locked onto water
Always being missed by his son, wife and daughter

Another day, another hour
But still gaining amounts of power
Another day, another death
Another dig, another breath

My dad's nose can always smell smoke
Mum has almost lost him, her heart almost broke
My dad's arms from digging are aching
He's still in the pit with his body shaking

Another day, another end
Another hour to extend
Finally he's finished the night
But he thinks about the next light.

Charlie Spencer (13)
Brannel School, St. Austell

A WORKING DAY

We wander up to this whimsical wood,
A path of milky water,
This blanket braced with spores.

When soon we hear a dig,
The footsteps of working men,
Soon a discovery is made,
A treasure for his life.

These boots with ancient souls,
The one who we see in the end,
Clay dug up and gone,
He blinks once, he blinks twice and trudges away.

What is left behind?
The digs that cry for home,
While all the streams search,
The work is done here.

Charlotte Lily Ross (12)
Brannel School, St. Austell

I AM ALONE

The harsh wind howls through the trees,
Green overtaking white.
A musty, earthy smell stretches over us.
The stillness is surrounding.
All that is left is the rushing of water.

Hollering, calling of friends
Friends saving each other's lives
There is the distant clang of the crib-calling bell
A time for everyone to reunite.

It has started
And something else has ended
War is calling all of us
And now I am alone.

Amelia Louvain Gardner (13)
Brannel School, St. Austell

THE PIT

Empty, abandoned, no one needs me,
But they do, I give them everything, they just need to dig deeper,
The life here is gone, I didn't mean to make them go away,
The scars hurt but it's okay just to feel the stomping of the men's feet on my soft layer of skin,
I wanted them to stay, but the machinery took over the jobs, the green, the air,
All the friendship has disappeared, been replaced with pain,
The thriving crib huts gone,
Sand slides too dangerous, knowing of death risen,
Wheels turning, pickaxes pounding, the sounds were comforting,
But now machinery running fills the memory with hatred,
I'm doomed to eternal sleep with no friends, no love, just work,
I tell myself no more death, no more clay.

Charley Julian (13)
Brannel School, St. Austell

SOMETHING IN NOTHING

In a moment when your heart is as
Empty as a ghostly battleground,
Yet bursting over the brim with
Nothing you could describe with
Nothing but a scream, or whimper.
You know you are fighting for
Your life and nothing else matters.

The only feelings you have are the ones
You can't name, and so you call them Nothing.
Everything else has shut down
And won't respond. You've become
A machine, a puppet, an imitation of life.
You aren't melodramatic. You aren't attention-seeking.
You're in pain. You're a fallen warrior.

You try to break yourself free and
Pick yourself up, but what help are they?
They demand you look up to them.
Respect and trust them, be like them.
Yet what effort do they make to listen
Without judging, to understand without controlling?
Better dead than like them.

It's a moment when you forget how to see
The light in life, you just don't know how.
You feel all the suffering of the world
As your own. You want them safe
But they're not, and who would listen
To what you wanted?

This is not some adolescent fairy tale
Because it's real, it's killing you.
And what do they do? Smother you with
Stigma and stereotypes and then wonder why
You feel so alone.
The only strength is that we find in each other.

If you were ten years older, fifteen years older,
Do you think they'd roll their eyes
And do everything they do?

In a moment when you damn everything
They want to hell, you realise you have to
Fight for yourself because no one else will.
You aren't weak. You aren't a failure.
You're better than them, you are not
What they think you are.

Phoebe Lake
Brighton Hove & Sussex Sixth Form College, Hove

IN EXTREMIS

My tears cascade, stream
Rivers of pollution and broken dreams
My skin rips at the seams
Quaking and drying out
Humanity is my gout
These are my griefs

Drills inject me, defecting me
Explosions scald me in the tenth degree
I accept my wounds silently
My complexion is scarred
Wilderness tamed, beauty marred
This is my sickness.

Sporadically I boil, erupt
They blame me for the disrupt
But it's them who are corrupt
I endure my agony
But my fury in magma weeps free
These are my screams

My affliction is these conditions
Asphyxiating on the emissions
Of ammunition, incineration
Incessantly, incandescently
Killing me.

Rhian Kane
Brighton Hove & Sussex Sixth Form College, Hove

THE GIRL

The girl sat there, with her head in her hands,
too scared to open her eyes, she longed to be back on land.
Images come and go, pounding in her mind,
and she wonders where she would be, if she had more time.
She remembers her family, of how they used to be,
but that was before the war, and before they had to flee.
She remembers her homeland, where she learned and where she grew,
but now it is torn apart, and there was nothing she could do.
She remembers her friends, the memories will never go.
Where are they now? That's what she wants to know.
She remembers that day, when her dad told her to run,
she didn't look back, and there was nothing she could have done.
She remembers when she grew tired, and she could no longer stand,
so she fell to the floor, and she fell asleep in the sand.
She remembers the hunger, the desperate thirst for a drink,
but she carried on walking, even though she couldn't see, hear or think.
She remembers when she saw the huts, she felt hope inside,
she wondered if they would help her, she was so happy that she cried.
She still remembers that place, and she remembers the scene,
blood had been spilled, lives had been lost and hope was nowhere to be seen.
She remembers walking further, and she remembers everything being wrong,
she remembers being lost, and there was nowhere she belonged.
But then there were shouts, voices, a hand,
she reached out, and she was taken far away from the sand.
And that's how she ended up here, far out at sea,
along with all the others, all of them trying to be free.
Free from the memories that came from hell,
memories that will become stories, which they shall tell.
Open your eyes, and can't you see?
These people are just like you and me.

Amy Jensen (13)
Chipping Campden School, Chipping Campden

THE END OF MY LIFE

I am shooting through the sky as if I am shooting across the sea,
The sky is empty and we are alone together,
The clouds are as white as unicorns and shoot love into your bleeding heart,
We are out of control, heading for the ends of our lives,
The passengers are all dead and we are the only ones left, my life will end in less than a minute.

Life is short and there is no way out of this,
We are in war and death is upon us, there is no way out and not even a way in.
My daughter is dead and my wife is lost,
My life has been torn apart as well as my heart.

People are still fighting and will still be fighting in Heaven,
When will this deathtrap come to an end?
We are now seconds away from the ground and everything is getting bigger and bigger as we get closer to death,
I don't know what to do, I don't want to lose my life today,
Today is my birthday not a day for death.

My life is such a mess and there is nothing I can do,
I wish there was a way out of this, but I know there is not,
Even if you could take time back a few steps,
And live those moments again.
My brother is a believer and will never give up,
He will survive, he can get through anything,
I don't believe in people that give up.
Two seconds to make a wish otherwise I will never see my life again,
But that wish I just cannot make,
Because someone else deserves it,
Someone who is risking their life for us.

I can't believe this was all a dream,
Death was never upon us
Please help . . .

James Philip Wheeler (13)
Chipping Campden School, Chipping Campden

HATE

Hate is something terrible in our souls,
It makes us feel incredibly cold.
It causes war and violence,
Why can't there ever be an alliance?
For war is cruel,
It's like a massive infinite duel.

Hate is something that will kill,
It can and will destroy everyone's will.
It fights against love, trying to turn it round,
But in the end everyone just falls down.
Screaming won't help on this level,
You'll never win because hate is the Devil.

Hate is something so very consuming,
When it enters it stays forever looming.
It never leaves you inside and out,
It's always in your mind, always talking at a shout.
The fact that it stays is just so terrifying,
It just feels so bad, electrifying.

Hate is so treacherous, so dangerous,
It's forever a burden which is ageless.
It overruns your mind and you forget love,
Soon in your eyes the end of the world comes from above.
If you try facing hate you'll end up out of breath,
And you'll be heading towards your death.

Hate is a virus in our hearts,
And it stays there till we part.
No way to escape, nowhere to hide,
No way to outrun this never-ending lie.
Death is all that lurks with hate
Ready to take you when it's just too late.

Daniella McCann (12)
Chipping Campden School, Chipping Campden

RESILIENCE

We are 3-0 down
I look like a clown
I tell the team 'heads up'
We need to win this cup
We are pushing forward
Now who is the coward?

A win would be like being able to ride a bike
Do we have a chance?

3-1, 3-2, 3-3
Expectations are high
We all have burning thighs
Finally our name will be on the map
All I can hear is sounds of claps

We aren't a bad team
But we can dream
Goal!
The final whistle blew
Did we just win, I have no clue
I scored the winning goal

The Queen just gave the cup
I think my jaw just dropped
My cheeks have gone red
Red as a tomato
All I can see is white lights
There's going to be a party tonight

A Premier League team getting beaten by a 2nd league team
It's just like a giraffe pacing out a tiger
Resilience.
'Keep on believing, never give up until the final whistle blows.'

Joshua John Angus (12)
Chipping Campden School, Chipping Campden

LEAVES

Crunch, crunch,
Us jumping on leaves,
Brown, red and yellow;
A rainbow,
Falling from trees.
Scrape, scrape,
Goes the rake,
Piling the leaves,
In a mini mountain.
'He he,' says me,
As I leap in the heap,
Leaves flying off the hill,
Some flowing to a windmill.
One after another we jump,
In the big lump,
Of leaves.

Amelia Jade Hancox (12)
Chipping Campden School, Chipping Campden

IN THE DEAD OF DARKNESS

In the dead of darkness,
the snow shimmers and plummets to the frost-plagued ground,
it shrieks, cries and glistens in the shimmering moonlight.
In the dead of darkness,
the emerald-green trees harbour the roosting birds, as they await the raging morning sun,
along with nocturnal beasts that dance among the black, lifeless forests.
In the dead of darkness,
the frost of the night crawls, and silently infects everything like a disease,
swarming like insects over every nook and cranny, and plaguing the world with its ice-cold blade.
In the dead of darkness.

Charlie Rainey (13)
Chipping Campden School, Chipping Campden

IN MY WINTER WONDERLAND

Water flowing through the crevices in my mind,
I wake up to the sound of tranquillity,
The white snow is all around me,
In my winter wonderland.

Everything is silent, still and smooth,
Like a diamond in the sky,
On a cold winter's night,
In my winter wonderland.

Winter is a time of happiness,
To spend with your family and friends,
Having a good time together,
In my winter wonderland.

New year is a time of celebration,
A time for new beginnings,
It is the time to look to the future,
In my winter wonderland.

Winter does not last forever,
Just like our hearts,
Be grateful for what you have,
In my winter wonderland.

Matthew Lear (13)
Chipping Campden School, Chipping Campden

THE POWER OF ANGER

Unleashed, untamed
Starts off with setting the spark
Then comes surviving the storm
Which has been hidden deep inside
And their heart roaring
Causing flames to rapidly build up
And then setting them free.

Ashley Adams (13)
Chipping Campden School, Chipping Campden

PEACE IN THE POPPY FIELD

The sun peaks over the hill so bright,
Ready to take away the night,
The wind blows and the little birds sing,
As the sun's rays pour through the trees,
And onto the crispy, auburn leaves.

The poppies sway gently in their field,
As bodies rest, their secrets sealed,
The bombs of war echo through the air,
And come crashing to the ground,
And kill all the innocent, some never found.

The river of blood as they fall to their feet,
But their loyalty meant Germans defeat,
Now they are free from the chaos of war,
Freedom the guns and rusty tanks,
To them England owes many thanks.

To some mysteries,
They may hold the key,
But let them rest
RIP.

Charlotte Victoria Burkert (11)
Chipping Campden School, Chipping Campden

PHOENIX FLYING FREE

Out of the ashes and into the snow,
A chained-up phoenix with nowhere to go.
Now having reached an all-time low,
As ye have reaped, so shall ye sow.

Now here's a phoenix with wings waiting to grow,
And now its looks are starting to show,
With red-gold plumage swathed on its back,
And a beak, so sharp, to defend from attack.

Here is a phoenix waiting to mate.
But the season is really, really quite late.
It swoops and it soars, but failing to find,
An eligible mate, one of its kind.
Yet look, in the air!
A mate-ready phoenix with nary a care!

That moment was pure beauty, such a sight to see,
The majestic beauty of a phoenix flying free.

Grace Royle (12)
Chipping Campden School, Chipping Campden

STARS

Isn't it funny?
The stars shine in the dark night sky,
Millions of stars, they have each other.
Beautifully dazzling in the gloomy dark sky,
The sky is instantly photogenic, like a big smile.
Now do you realise?
Family is much like stars.
They brighten up the darkest days when you feel the emptiest inside,
Giving you a little sparkle in your heart.
Your melancholy frown transforms into the joyous smile of happiness,
Instantly ready for a camera out of nowhere.
In the light of the day, stars do not shine,
However they are there.
Just like family,
They may not always be present with you
But you always know they are there for you.

Emily May Ellison (12)
Chipping Campden School, Chipping Campden

UMBRELLAS IN THE RAIN

When the rain falls,
And people run.
When candles flicker,
And men reap fear.

We all hide ourselves away,
We all are cowards underneath,
We wish ill intent,
And cry tears of anguish.

The pain of others we hide away.
We wear our masks of logic,
And hide our hearts of stone,
When faced with problems we cannot resolve . . .

We shun away,
Protect ourselves,
We are all umbrellas in the rain.

Eliot Reaney (14)
Chipping Campden School, Chipping Campden

THE DREAM!

The waves are rolling in and out,
and I really don't want to hang about
The wind is coming,
and I should be running!
The sand is getting into my eyes,
it's like I can see some crazy spies.
My teeth are chattering,
and my hands are shivering.
I really want to go home,
to give my dog a bone.
Something is in the distance,
can anyone help me, I need assistance!

I am starting to sweat,
Come on Milly, don't get in a fret!
I am really scared now!
Did I just hear a miaow?

Is this a dream?
What's this about working in a team?
I am getting my words all jumbled up,
Plus I do feel the only way is up!
The waves are coming up to my feet,
Like it is some sort of meet and greet!
I am now starting to wobble and suddenly,
I am back in my bed, but I am standing on my head!

Milly Nixon (11)
Chipping Campden School, Chipping Campden

SPRING TO WINTER

The chunky rusty latch
the crumbling, crunching thatched roof;
a slithering serpent like a dithering tortoise,
rough and tough.
Lacklustre clusters,
squirming selectively: sweet-scented saffron shivers.
Grass glimmers glamorously; he gazes intently.
He was so thoughtful, he could have drifted away.
Birds buzz and bees sing like a beautiful cacophony of instruments.
The twinkling day core beats rapidly
and highlights the opening day
into a blizzard of fresh hay.
The twittering and tweeting, alongside the drizzling rain
yelps and cries through bitter tastes.
The leaves all sob with relief, the trees swaying joyfully.
Like a sizzling fire to swirling whirlpools:
The seasons are too cruel to be kind.
Spring grieves painfully but beautifully.
Until she falls and winter arrives,
coating the flowers with a thick blanket of snow.
Floating snowflakes cheer happily.
The olive ocean of ice gleams,
sparkles and shimmers softly
like a faint light beam.
Slippery sleet: soft and slushed, spread all over the smooth, chilled roads.
Thick sheets of sleek glass: he snaps and cracks crossly.
That he could have ripped it in two with the bark of soulless hands.

Too peaceful to be touched: too gorgeous to be scorned.
Winter is most wonderful!

Molly D'Ayala (12)
Didcot Girls' School, Didcot

HATEFUL AND HOPEFUL

Hate,
A bitter word always spat with venom.

Hate,
A word so strong that even the Devil's heart weeps.

Hate,
Every letter surrounds you, concealing you in a bubble of darkness.

Hate,
A feeling even the bravest fear.

Hate... is just a word,
But Hope means something.

Hope,
Shatters Hate into blunt black shards.

Hope,
Is what makes a man,
Not what destroys him!

Hope,
Is what dulls the pain of Hate and gives us the courage to carry on
Loving our friends and family,
And even the people who sell their souls to Hate and Cruelty
Are still influenced by Hope!

Hope,
Is that little spark in our heart
That carries on shining even at the darkest of times.

Niamh Payne (13)
Didcot Girls' School, Didcot

UNDER THE RIVER WILL MAKE YOU SHIVER ...

River, river,
rapid river,
can you slither,
and make me shiver,
shiny and cold,
but very old,
are you made of gold?
Lost your soul,
shrunk deep, dark, glossy coat of sea,
underneath lays a mystery!

Alanna Galley (12)
Didcot Girls' School, Didcot

MAYBE IT'S HER TIME . . .

I want you to live forever
But I know it's not true
You will die one day
And that's not new.

We knew this day was coming
We hoped not this soon
You know not how long you have
But it always comes too soon.

We thought he would be first
But now he's had his burst
I don't think he knows it
But somewhere inside
He knows it's not alright.

You might not know
But we break down
Often or so.

Maybe it's her time . . .
Maybe she will be happier
Maybe she will laugh
Maybe she will miss us
Maybe she will miss our home
But for sure *I* know
I will be missing her more
No matter where she goes.

Caitlin Taylor (14)
Elmfield Rudolf Steiner School, Stourbridge

WHEN DID THE CHILDREN STOP SINGING?

When did the children stop singing?
Where did the sunny days go?
Why have the people stopped listening?
What happened to playing in the snow?

When did the trees start dying?
Where did the red leaves go?
Since when did the skies get so grey?
Why don't the flowers still grow?

When did the laughter stop echoing?
Where did the fun times go?
Why can't we just start living?
How come the answer's still no?

When did my mind start wandering?
Where did the normal things go?
Why am I thinking so deeply?
About pain and sadness and sorrow?

When did the children stop singing?
Where did the sunny days go?
It pains me to write this poem,
I just thought that you should know.

Francesca Hall (15)
Elmfield Rudolf Steiner School, Stourbridge

GOING HOME

There is always a journey in a person's life
For me it starts at my grandma's house
It usually begins with a hurried goodbye
Then a walk to a leafy dead end
After a small delay the bus rumbles by
At the top of the bus you can see the rush
As you get onto the high street's crush
After what seems like a few moments
Baker Street you're there
A brisk walk to the station so you can jump
On in celebration
The melancholy hits after a moment
Or two, watching the capital fly away from you
Bicester North and Banbury, Leamington Spa
The stations pass away then get further afar
A panic sets in; there's homework!
Oh well, I will do it some other time
Soon outside, there is darkness
Yellow lights flicker as we get quicker and quicker
The day draws closer to an end
Don't worry, I will soon be in the capital again.

Gabriel Brothers (15)
Elmfield Rudolf Steiner School, Stourbridge

FANTASY WORLDS

Walking through woods
Where all is bright and good
Creatures, plants and scents of all kinds
Can be imagined with only one person's mind.

First the scene is plain as can be
Then, out of nowhere, pops up a banshee
With nought but a thought everything can change
To something weird, wonderful and strange.

A feast with the gods, against all the odds
Travelling through space in shuttles or pods
Battling an army whilst wearing a dress
Defeating a dragon for a damsel in distress.

All can be imagined, experienced and felt
Like going to Hogwarts and casting a spell
Become a villain, feel their pain
Create a tragic back story, leave nothing the same.

But at the end of the day
It will all fall away
Leaving you to feel sad and empty.

Tara de Wit (15)
Elmfield Rudolf Steiner School, Stourbridge

HOME

Laugh and the world laughs with you
Weep and you weep alone
For the modern girl
Who feels alone
Is looking for a home.

She sits there feeling lonely
Looks to men who seem holy
She just needs the comfort
Even if it gets her hurt
These people are so cold.

Four walls is not enough
This world is just so tough
She just can't lay in his arms enough
Even if he's kinda rough.

She just sits and weeps alone at night
This terrible feeling isn't right
Off she sets into the night
Trying to sort this messed-up life.

Zakya Leila Paraiso (15)
Elmfield Rudolf Steiner School, Stourbridge

MY INNER CHILD

Where have you been my inner child
playing in the rain outside?
You shouldn't be here at this time of night
when you know it isn't right.

Have you realised that things have changed at last
alone in the crowd
People moving too fast
wake up to your shout

To broken toys on the floor
that Daddy won't pick up anymore.

Franka Roese (15)
Elmfield Rudolf Steiner School, Stourbridge

SUN

I give you the sun,

to heat the warmth in your heart,
Spread the heat round the
circle of love,

don't let the clouds take,
it away
Shine through what you love

take the rays of light, let
it run free

be bright and powerful

stay strong through what
you believe,

I say please don't let
the clouds take
it away.

Tara Tustin (14)
Elmfield Rudolf Steiner School, Stourbridge

JUST BECAUSE

Just because I'm 15, doesn't mean I'm not important to society,
Just because I'm a girl doesn't mean I'm weak,
Just because I love ballet doesn't mean I don't have legs like a
football player,
Just because I'm gay doesn't mean I'm not human,
Just because I go to a private school doesn't mean I'm posh,
Just because I like rock music doesn't mean I think all genres are
rubbish,
Just because I haven't got a lot of friends doesn't mean I'm not happy,
It's quality not quantity.
Just because!

Riannon Parsons (15)
Elmfield Rudolf Steiner School, Stourbridge

MURDER IN THE MORNING

Blood is red
Bruises are blue
I am dead
And now so are you.

I'll come for you in the morning
I don't want to find you snoring
Be up and ready for me to take you away
To an unknown land
Where I'll lead you astray
I'll do it with grace
No pain will be felt
I'll hang you from your neck
Just using my belt.

Libby Clarke (14)
Elmfield Rudolf Steiner School, Stourbridge

PLAGIARISM

In an English class on a Friday gone
The whole class was told by Mrs Underwood
To each write a poem
It had better be good.

As I struggled to write an adequate rhyme
Plagiarism crossed my mind, but no, it had to be my own
With literary devices we had been shown.

Aliteration, AAA, metaphors as high as the sky
The use of antithesis be they good or bad
The, the, the use, use, use, of, of, of, tricolon, tricolon, tricolon.

This is my poem, a bit of a story
I hope you like it.

Jake Woodley (15)
Elmfield Rudolf Steiner School, Stourbridge

LOOK

We look here
We look there
We look everywhere
Is it just me
Is this what we
Should see?
Is it life
Is it right
Is this what my
Eyes should see?
Can this really be
The correct
Place for me?

Tara Tustin (14)
Elmfield Rudolf Steiner School, Stourbridge

WHY?

Why is it that when we have to go to school,
We have to meet the standards they need?
The standards they need to say that they are the the best school in our area.
Why meet the standards when everybody is different?
Everybody is different on the inside and out.
Why do we have to be the same?
Why do we need good grades?
Why do we follow the rules?
We follow the rules and are the same,
All because society tells us we have to be.

Olivia Bell (15)
Elmfield Rudolf Steiner School, Stourbridge

HELL

Blood-red, curdling cries
Frightened faces, burning fire.
Welcome to Hell. Not your heart's desire,
But enjoy the blood gushing,
It's our waterfall.

Blood-red, curdling cries
Fallen hopes and battle cries.
Welcome to Hell, you'll be here forever.
Don't try to leave,
It'll just make things harder.

Tyler Macdonald (14)
Elmfield Rudolf Steiner School, Stourbridge

JUST BECAUSE

Just because I'm by myself, doesn't mean I'm alone
Just because I sleep for hours, doesn't mean I won't be tired
Just because I'm different, doesn't make me bad
Just because I say inside, doesn't mean I have no life
Just because I'm finding myself, doesn't mean I don't have my own two feet
Just because I watch kids' movies, doesn't make me a child
Just because I don't see beauty in myself, doesn't mean I don't see it in everyone else
Just because I say I hate you, doesn't mean I mean it.

Jemima Buckland (14)
Elmfield Rudolf Steiner School, Stourbridge

DAYBREAK

The sun cast its first gold rays;
Creeping fast, on the sky line.
Revealing the dark, quiet lake;
And the soft, white clouds above.
Filled, by this beauty and warmth,
Now I hear the freedom call.
And my wings, suddenly unfold.
It is high time to enjoy;
This gift, nature granted me.
Carried by the wind I fly . . .

Déborah Hayat (14)
Elmfield Rudolf Steiner School, Stourbridge

ONIONS

Onions are like love
Like the moon from above
They are white and in a circle

They have light brown skin
And it's not very thin
But it protects it from being damaged

They make you cry like love
And die like love
If you are allergic to onions!

George Hayes (15)
Elmfield Rudolf Steiner School, Stourbridge

WHAT IS WAR?

Marching men, off to war,
Fine young soldiers, boys no more.
Honour and glory, pride for the nation,
Striding on, with anticipation.

Dark skies, shrill screams,
Lying, groaning, horrific dreams.
Bombs and bullets whistle past,
Constantly coming, thick and fast!

Attack, attack, attack!
No way back!
The horrors of the trench,
And the rats with their stench.
One by one, shot to the ground,
Some, never to be found.

A shout, a roar, up they burst!
Charging through the battlefields,
Drenched in thirst.
To kill a German, their only mission,
And rid the world of evil ambition.

Death and disease surround me now,
With scars and sorrow upon my brow.
Injured and tired, crippled and sore,
The pain and the fear, of this dreadful war.

All alone in a foreign field,
A frightened soldier with no shield,
'If I should die, remember me,
War no more . . . let it be.'

Yasmin Parsons (14)
Focus School Knockloughrim Campus, Magherafelt

THE MYSTERIOUS MAGICIAN

The mysterious magician
had one ambition.
To make everyone disappear
to everywhere but here!

He owned a top hat
and an invisible cat.
Friendly and mysterious
mischievous yet serious!

We were all in shock
when he escaped from that lock.
No one will ever know
how he performed his show.

The mysterious magician, known far and wide
until that day when he sadly died.
To all he brought laughter and joy
inexplicable magic, was his toy!

Austin Hughes (11)
Focus School Knockloughrim Campus, Magherafelt

MEMORY OF MY CAT – BUFFY

Walking in a circle,
Is what she likes to do,
She's blind and deaf,
But still finds her way through.

Miaowing constantly,
All day and night,
She wouldn't notice,
If she was on a flight.

Her name is Buffy,
She hurt her eyes in a fight,
Her ears went up to Heaven,
And all she can do is bite.

Tasmin Rhiannon Sproson (13)
Fowey River Academy, Fowey

OH DAUGHTER OF MINE

Oh daughter
of mine, what
happened to you? Your
supple skin burned
and your lips
turned blue.
Oh daughter
of mine, how much
shall I pay? To make
such an ugly complexion go
away? For through your eyes you can
not see and with such a face
what will your future
be? Oh daughter of
mine, we'll make a
twin, kill it for the
treasures it hides and
at last we may put
our troubled minds
at ease. Oh sweet
girl, yes, daughter
of mine, your
innocent heart,
so pure, divide.
The replacement
face has touched
your soul, for
which, I
am sorry,
I fear my
actions shall take
their toll. My love,

forgive me, oh daughter
of mine, for killing the girl
you held so high. She
possessed your face,
your body, but not
your mind. Oh daughter
I hope I can still call
you mine. I watched
you cry and part of myself
did die. As you reached
for the clone's
skin upon your cheek.
I turned from a
girl who shrieked
and shrieked.

Millie Sheen (14)
Fowey River Academy, Fowey

PARENTS

Every time they say, 'Go to your room!'
And, 'Think about what you've done!'
I get annoyed and blinded with rage
And say, 'What are you thinking, Dad or Mum?'

I say it's unfair, but they've got a good reason for this
There's no need to get my knickers in a twist!
I sit on my bed and think they're really dumb
I say, 'What are you thinking, Dad or Mum?'

Every minute of every day I get chores galore
For once I would like the break that I'm looking for
I think they don't care if I'm feeling glum
I say, 'What are you thinking, Dad or Mum?'

Now that I've calmed down I finally see
That it's all my fault for being so fussy
And in the end I know they care for me
No matter what I do, or who I be.

Jed Gwilliams (12)
Fowey River Academy, Fowey

MY ROLO-BEAR

From Polruan he came
(he once was a stray)
Purring into our lives
With a swish and a sway.

His coat's brown and black
With a tabby-like sheen
Big belly, caramelly
And eyes of lime-green.

His heart is humongous
His brain's not so big
He's lovely but lazy
And a bit of a pig!

He's always quite hungry
. . . thinks teatime's at three!
Only braving the rain
To go out for a wee.

Food fills his dreams
He's a big ball of fluffy
He sleeps through the day
When he plays he goes puffy.

He stares out the window
Whilst dreaming of Dreamies
He sneaks out at night
Always thinking up schemies.

He arrived on my birthday
Back when I was nine
Best birthday cat ever!
So glad he was mine!

He gets squished in the catflap
Then his bum wriggles free
He's the best ever bear-cat
Don't you agree?

Jacob Luck (12)
Fowey River Academy, Fowey

THIS IS THE FUTURE AS I SEE IT

Facebook, Instagram, Snapchat and Twitter
A dumping ground full of social litter
Staring at tablets and mobile devices
A place people need to share all their vices
This is the future as I see it.

A society of robots, blinking at screens
I must update my status by any means
My latest profile pic, a selfie divine
For some reason taking this many photos of myself is fine
This is the future as I see it.

I want to succeed and get a good job
But mobile devices are turning me into a slob
I spend my time talking to a laptop screen
When I should be out on the grass lush and green
This is the future as I see it.

Our legacy no more than USB plug sockets
Certainly not a generation creating space rockets
Losing the skills to interact with anyone new
Leaving our Internet-free friends to be few
This is the future as I see it.

In the past we would meet with friends after school
Now if you're away from the computer you're not cool
A future of crooked necks and hand strains
Are we really heading into a world of social media pains
This is the future as I see it.

It won't be zombies, earthquakes or knives
Not 'World's End' caused by nagging husbands or wives
Our ignorance of others and addiction to media
A society based on 'likes' has made us all needier
This is the future as I see it.

Shauna Lee Nicholas (15)
Fowey River Academy, Fowey

LET ME BE ME

Don't tell me what I can and can't be,
I am not a doll, a dog or robot.
I am youth, a youngster, I'm wild.
I cannot be contained or controlled,
I do as I please, I'm free.
Don't set unrealistic goals,
Ones I can never achieve,
Just let me be me.

If I'm gay, if I'm straight,
Who are you to hate?
I've never met you, befriended you,
I couldn't care less what you think.
So leave me be, I'm fine, living life in peace.
I don't need bullies, racists or homophobics.
I'm happy as I am, give me a chance,
We teens, we need room to breathe,
Just let me be me.

So what if I can't calculate in my head,
Or spend days in bed?
I can write, draw, dance and sing.
I may not be good at science, but I am doing something.
I'm not on the streets, doing drugs, or so what if I am?
It's what I want, it's my choice, I'll make it right in the end.
We're children not sinners, it's part of growing up,
Making mistakes and fixing them again.
You say we'll grow up, then give us the time,
We've made our choices, so let us run wild.
Give us space, time and love,
It's not a phase sometimes but it's what we want.
Respect that, don't end that, just let me be me.

Meghan Coon (14)
Fowey River Academy, Fowey

BEING LENNON

Spotty face and wispy hairs,
Staring back at my handsome face,
I guess my character is my saving grace,
Always feeling that I'm not good enough,
The only way to get through is by a smile and a bluff,
Always rules: do this, do that.
When I don't tuck my shirt in,
Get a detention and life falls flat.
Mr Dale, our new head, just four words he'll say to me,
'Tuck in your shirt!
A detention for you, then you'll see!'
Is that all Mr Dale sees, a scruffy young lout?
'There's more to Lennon inside!'
I want to shout!
Just leave me alone!
Life as a teen, it's hard can't you see!
But you can't remember can you?
Because you're 43!
Trying to fit in when you're ginger and tall,
When you are seen as different,
Life isn't a ball,
But to all on the outside,
I appear chilled and laid back,
But sometimes on the inside,
I feel like I'm gonna crack,
Adults say it gets easier,
But as a teen, life is hard,
The things that we go through, can leave you feeling scarred,
So all you grown-ups give us a break,
Cos you don't see our insides and all the heartache.

Lennon Ashton Retallick (14)
Fowey River Academy, Fowey

REALITY

Keep your head up
Stand tall
Don't look around
It doesn't matter anymore
Uncover your ears
There's nothing left to fear
The gunshots are gone
It's only crying you hear
Wipe away your tears
Keep them close to your heart
Just keep running
I'm sorry you'll have to be apart
Dig down, dig deep
There's a long way to go
I know you just want to weep
But there's something to show
The truth
The truth of fear
The truth of suffering
The truth of pain
I'm sorry for your fear
I'm sorry for your suffering
I'm sorry for your pain
You've been broken
You've been hurt
This is the truth
This is our reality
Just because it isn't happening to you
Doesn't mean it isn't happening at all.

Charlotte Trinckvel (13)
Fowey River Academy, Fowey

MY FUTURE

My future has yet to be written
I have no idea what will be
But in my dreams
It's a wonderful place
A place I can't wait to see.

Travel will be in an instant
Transporters instead of cars
No longer a plane ride
To sunnier shores
Just a five-second transfer to Mars.

Technology gets even smarter
A computer inside of my head
No more gaming
With silly old handsets
Just virtual gaming instead.

In the future there won't just be humans
There'll be robots just like me and you
And alien pals
From worlds far away
Will be part of our families too.

So my future has yet to be written
But I hope this is how it will be
No longer a dream
But an actual place
A place I'll be happy to see.

Daniel Smith (11)
Fowey River Academy, Fowey

THE EVOLUTION OF WAR

In the beginning there was nothing,
no morals, no friendship, not a thing,
then war came about and ruined the little that they had,
Making so many sad,
war is unbelievably bad.

With swords they fought,
death is what past soldiers sought,
killing everything they saw,
sometimes war needed to be but most broke a moral law,
war is unbelievably bad.

We haven't learnt much have we?
Machine guns and fear,
can't people see?
War is wrong, so why can't we settle it and cheer,
war is unbelievably bad.

What does the future hold?
Do we face destruction?
Which countries will fall?
Can't people live happily?
War is unbelievably bad.

I hope that war ceases,
and happiness increases,
Then maybe we won't fall to pieces,
because if we do there will be nothing left to ruin,
war is unbelievably bad.

Bethany Patricia Ayres (15)
Fowey River Academy, Fowey

THE DAY OF A RACE

It's 6am
The day of a race
A tough course ahead
I have to face

The training I've done
Is about to show
How well I can do
I'll try not to slow

And now at the start
I begin to panic
When off goes the gun
As if by magic

Up and down
Around I go
Through mud, in rain
It's hard, I know

Up comes the finish
What a great feeling
The last final stretch
I'm almost squealing

Now I am done
I'm happy to see
My coaches, my teammates
Smiling at me.

Rhianna Giles (14)
Fowey River Academy, Fowey

DARK CLOUDS

Dark clouds
no light
The sunshine has gone
people
point and giggle
push and shove
as I go past
or, sit in class
name-calling
'Geek'
'Weird boy'
'Speccy four-eyes'
'Weirdo'
School bag hidden
possessions taken
chair kicked
whispering
behind my back
a friend
with a smile
nice things said
Dark clouds
become white
light peeps through
sunshine
I will get through this.

Toby Harris (14)
Fowey River Academy, Fowey

6 MONTHS 9 DAYS

You held me close as we said goodbye
I could feel the tears from your eyes

I wish it didn't end like this
I can't even remember our last kiss
I wanted to hear those words escape your lips
It was all just a trick
It made me sick

I left your side and tried to keep my pride
I just think about all the lies
I cried every night, wishing
I could win this fight with my mind

Don't try and find me
I'm just a runaway, a danger to society
And soon a memory

This won't escape me
I want the pain to leave me
the mark you leave is the mark of slavery

Your words, they drown me
In the venom you throw at me
You tell me I'm living in a fantasy

I wish you would leave me
The walls keep changing in this life you've made for me
Now, you've changed me, you won't bury me.

Jenna Newcombe (14)
Fowey River Academy, Fowey

A POEM FOR MY BROTHER

My dad had a son before my mum married him,
So I had an older brother, I looked up to him,
He was a clever chappie, ten O levels to his name,
He went to work at 'Tulips', a manager he became.

He really loved the river, where he'd go fishing with our dad,
Standing on the riverbank with rods in their hands,
Who could catch the biggest fish, they would debate,
Photo taken, cooked or smoked, then served on a plate.

One day he met a special girl, his head was in a spin,
He wondered, if he asked, would she marry him,
They both agreed and set a date, I was very happy,
A bridesmaid I would be with sandals, high and strappy.

Fourteen days before the wedding my brother became ill,
But he hadn't been to the doctors to get any pills,
He thought it was a cold you see and went home to keep warm,
But suddenly got worse as the evening wore on.

He was rushed to hospital after an ambulance was rung,
While he fought for his life trying to hang on,
Sadly he didn't make it, I miss him to this day,
He had meningitis but he fought and was brave.

They say the good ones go first, in this case it's true,
Just to let you know that I never will forget you.

Lauren White (14)
Fowey River Academy, Fowey

SOCIAL MEDIA

Everyone's always looking down, never up.
Everyone stays in touch through a screen.
What happened to a hello instead of a friend request?
What happened to the world that used to gleam?

What happened to friends instead of stalkers?
What happened to innocence?
Meaning always lost in codes
Friendships always lost in messages.

'Stranger Danger' is hidden by Internet best friends.
Cyberbullies hidden in fake profiles.
Likes on Facebook is better than likes in real life.
Comments on Instagram is all the world needs.

Tweets? Like Twitter?
Notes? Like Tumblr?
Kick? Like Kik?
Stories? Like Snapchat?

Ten-second pictures with a cruel message.
I need a screenshot.
A picture you don't like, posted.
I need to comment.

We live in a world of social media.
Social media meaning addiction.

Lillie Bamsey (14)
Fowey River Academy, Fowey

UNTITLED

When I look into the future I see robotic trees,
And they no longer make me sneeze,
When I look to the left I see flying cars,
When I look to the right I see Mars.

I smell the air, it's heavy with pollution,
Caused by the technical evolution,
The air is full of fumes,
That I still consume.

I still hear the engines,
It seems weird with things flying around,
Electric travel still has not been found,
I do like the flying sounds.

Fast food restaurants are everywhere,
Coffee shops, here and there,
Nobody likes to share,
Supermarkets spoil the view.

It feels dark and gloomy,
I liked the sunny days,
With the sun rays,
And the flowers blooming,
I'd like to change the future that I see,
To the past that was lived in.

Dillon Cooper (11)
Fowey River Academy, Fowey

LIFE IS GREAT

Life is great,
Not to be detested.
You can do what you want . . .
As long as you're not arrested.

You could go to a city,
Have a blast!
But make sure you don't,
End up an outcast.

You can find love,
Which is such a treat.
But then find out your
Partner's a cheat.

As long as you're happy,
Is what they say.
But it's hard to keep,
Depression at bay.

Life can suck,
It's unfair.
But getting through it,
Isn't too much to bear.

Hannah Abbiss (14)
Fowey River Academy, Fowey

LIVING ENTERTAINMENT

The feeling of enslavement,
trapped in a cage,
what the human race is doing,
they are not meant to be on a stage.

The sound of a whale cry,
the sight of a motionless fox,
the smell of a bull's corpse,
as it lies in discourse.

The training of a lion,
a regal animal,
enslaved and beaten,
in a circus scandal.

The howl of a mutt,
that had lost a fight,
as the drunken owner,
screamed in the flickering streetlight.

So just stop and think,
is this animal containment,
because what we are watching,
is living entertainment.

Jess Cottrell (12)
Fowey River Academy, Fowey

OUR FUTURE

Nuclear power, what have you done?
To have the world on the run.
Space, universe our only hope
How will children cope?
Time and love will tell
If we can break this warring spell.

Max Martin Isbell (11)
Fowey River Academy, Fowey

WHAT IS IT LIKE TO BE A TEENAGER IN TODAY'S SOCIETY?

When she was at her lowest she didn't shed a tear,
She simply sat and watched the rain patter dismally at her window,
The darkness slowly drowned her,
As her demons learnt to swim,
Her internal screams growing louder from within,
The dreams she dreamt as a little girl became nothing more than thoughts,
As the stroke of a match and deep inhale made her question what was real,
She counted the many times she had prayed for a glimmer of hope,
A haven for her mind, for it had turned so frail,
I stand before an array of desks,
Education captivating the young minds,
In a society where you must be your best at all times,
It's hard to stay in line,
My future here is hard to vision,
Reality and expectations will soon have a collision,
After all, nobody really cares unless you're clever, pretty or dying,
'I'm fine, I'll keep trying,' we say
But inside? We're crying.

Mollie Story (14)
Fowey River Academy, Fowey

IMAGINE

Imagine a world where I didn't have to do injections every day.
Imagine a world where I didn't have to check my blood sugar levels all the time.
Imagine a world where I could eat anything without worrying.
Technology would make sure none of this affected me or anyone else.
Technology could change our lives for the better.
Imagine a world without Type 1 diabetes.
Wouldn't that make a great future?

Molly Winch (14)
Fowey River Academy, Fowey

SMALL STEPS

We all have to face many things that scare us throughout our lives . . .
They aren't always as bad as they seem
Small steps . . .
Face your fears, no need for tears

You can be anything you want to be if only you have the imagination
New adventures are always worthwhile you see
You never know you might just have some fun
Small steps . . .
Face your fears, no need for tears

Everything happens for a reason
We all make mistakes
Grow from it, learn from it, move on
Small steps . . .
Face your fears, no need for tears

Be courageous, have strength
Live without regret
Always follow your heart
Small steps,
Face your fears, no need for tears.

Kelsie Jeffreys (11)
Fowey River Academy, Fowey

WEATHER, WEATHER

The wind is howling,
the snow is falling,
and all the trees are bare,
in the distance the sun appears,
brightening up the air.

The wind is cold,
the snow is thick,
but over there, in the heart,
no one has to care.

Poppy Hawke (12)
Fowey River Academy, Fowey

THE LITTLE SAILOR

Tilted on its side,
worn, ill and waiting
to be revived,
for ten years it
had been 'Asi',
denied, rejected and
alone,
A bullied vessel of
beauty, I'm sure,
It shone light
on me and the
same vice versa,
it was to be
restored before
the dawn of
'primavera',
to achieve, to become,
but most of all to find
its way into the little
sailor's heart . . .

Henry Chapman (12)
Fowey River Academy, Fowey

WHAT IT'S LIKE BEING ME

OMG, it's great being me,
It's such fun just to hang out in my own company,
Doing things I CBA, like homework, it's such a chore,
And I find it such a bore,
Why I ask myself,
Surely homework is bad for my health,
Instead what makes me happy,
Is sleeping till noon,
Oblivious to the world outside, safe and warm where I can hide,
Until feeding time arrives.

Jake Butler (14)
Fowey River Academy, Fowey

FUELLED BY NATURE

Green trees
and coloured guards
birds and bugs
playing cards
water dripping
happiness forming
love and trust
hearts warming
spoke too soon
a man-made devil
for above this bliss
a horror shaped from metal
the force was too strong
they were helpless
Mankind's greed
had left them defenceless . . .
black trees
and coloured water
remains and bones
complete slaughter . . .

Maisie Colwill (12)
Fowey River Academy, Fowey

THE FUTURE

The future is a mystery
The only thing certain is history
The time will keep ticking
As the world keeps spinning
The future is unpredictable
As the past is left behind
Live each day with that in mind
Each day just be kind
Then maybe you will find your future is inside.

Adam Lamarti (12)
Fowey River Academy, Fowey

IN ONE HUNDRED YEARS' TIME

Will cars be automatic?
Will houses clean themselves?
Will robots do everything for us?
Will smart phones be even smarter?

But how will the world cope with a growing population?
Will we have trouble making enough food and water?
Will there be any green land left?
Will everyone get along so there are no more wars?

But maybe we will be able to make the things we dream of,
Maybe we will travel to other planets,
Maybe we will have found cures for diseases,
Maybe technology will develop beyond anything we can imagine.

One hundred years is a long way off but during that time,
We will discover new things,
Scientists will make incredible developments,
There is still so much for us to learn.

We have to take every opportunity to make the world a better place,
So who knows how the world will be in one hundred years' time.

Elliot Toms (11)
Fowey River Academy, Fowey

EMOTIONS

A pinch of anxiety
A hint of sadness
A bucket of joy
A waterfall of happiness
A fragment of anger
A grain of disgust
A parcel of surprise
A lorry load of love
This makes us human.

Tobias Pascoe (12)
Fowey River Academy, Fowey

THE FUTURE – MY PAST, PRESENT, MY FUTURE

My world is changing
I go to pre-school, without my mum
Why does she leave me?
I learn to play with others, to colour, to count
I have fun, I enjoy it.

Another change, I go to primary school
My days are filled with all the things I must know
I play sport; rugby, cricket and football
I am part of a team, we grow as a team, we win as a team
No sooner am I accustomed than it's time to move on.

To secondary school, I must go
To learn more about the things I must know
To help me to develop and grow
What will I be? I don't know
But what I have been given is a chance, an opportunity
To prepare me for a future, what will that be?
Nobody knows.

Lewis Ovens (12)
Fowey River Academy, Fowey

FOREVER

The sky isn't the colour of the sea anymore
The leaves don't fall as red anymore
Darkness isn't the absence of light anymore
Forests aren't full of just animals anymore
Finally asleep isn't safe anymore
Losing someone you love isn't sad anymore
The dying don't leave once they're dead anymore
The dead stay with you now
Forever.

Talia Lewis-Fowler (14)
Fowey River Academy, Fowey

WHAT MAKES ME ANGRY

I was asked to write a poem.
And it also needed to include what makes me angry.
I know what makes me angry: creating poems.
That makes me really angry.
It's hard to structure a poem;
It makes me really angry.
Also loads of homework, which consists of creating poems.
This also makes me angry.
And trying to add ABAB rhymes into my poems.
It's frustrating and makes me really angry.
And trying to add enjambment into my poems, it's
irritating and it makes me really angry.
It's also hard to add onomatopoeia into poems.
It makes my brain pop and it makes me angry.
It's also hard to add rhymes if you're a poet.
Actually I'm quite good at it, I just didn't know it.
It's also hard to add colloquialisms into my poem,
My anger for this technique is out of this world.
But repetition, repetition it's easy.

Ethan Salt (14)
Fowey River Academy, Fowey

BOREDOM

Nothing to do,
What should I do?
What would you do?
Is it the right thing to do?
Something I would never do?
Something I would maybe do,
Definitely maybe not,
Ties my stomach in a knot,
Could you not?
Should I?
Should I not?

Josh Bateman (13)
Fowey River Academy, Fowey

MY LIFE

I am not precisely similar nor do I find it proficient to be like others,
I can sometimes be steady like the ticking of a clock, or fragile like glass,
I would spend time worrying about each second of the day, and fearing what my mind might conjure up next.
The questioning of why I am like I am and the bother of the world around me, is deafening.
If I had to describe in one word what it's like to be me, the word would be 'unrelatable', at most.
Though I am a person like others, and my interests can be a relatable thing, my experience of day-to-day life and mind is highly unrelatable.
The loss of the silence, the unsteadiness, can only be understood by myself alone.
My indefinable world, which can't be understood in full detail by many, feels unfrequented.
The vacuous assemblage that stores my being forever stays as divider of my true reminiscence.

Aaleyah Bate (14)
Fowey River Academy, Fowey

THE CHOCOLATE RACE

Our planet is sick and gasping for breath and all of the humans are thinking about death.
One day we will colonise Mars and then everybody will get free chocolate bars.
Then we will have to take over Snickers and this will feed all the chocolate pickers.
This will make humanity quite porky and so we have to be cautious on the planet of Yorkie.
Chocolate monsters will be found in the swamps of Picnic, Lion, Topic and Chomps.
But the strength of the human race will be crippled under the power of the mighty Galaxy Ripple.

Archie Gwilliams (14)
Fowey River Academy, Fowey

MEMORIES THAT STAY FOREVER

Even though you aren't here no more
You will never leave my many memories
I still wish you were here
But your spirit still lives on inside

All your odd habits still make me think
I hear a cry at the door
Or jump towards me when I drop
Some tasty food on the clear floor
We still go round with food
The bowl used to be empty, now it's full
And I miss your friendly 'hello'
When I walk through the door

Although you used to bring in new friends
And more food to eat
That one place in my heart
Belongs to you . . . and always will
No matter what.

Charlotte Pennington (13)
Fowey River Academy, Fowey

UNTITLED

Cascading leaves fall to the ground,
All orange, red and rusty brown,
Whistling wind blowing a breeze,
Creaking and swaying all the trees,
Blue sky above but the air is fresh,
Hats and scarves, maybe a thermal vest!
The smell of spring not far away,
Oh, how I miss long, sunny day,
Soon the nights will be light again,
Back to BBQs in the evening with friends,
But for now on this autumn day
I *shall* enjoy the things I see on my way.

Sophie Hodson (14)
Fowey River Academy, Fowey

AS A YOUNG CARER

As a young carer, I care for my dad,
Some days are good, some days are bad.
It takes up a lot of my time,
But I do it, instead of whine.

As a young carer, what really angers me
Is 'normal' teenagers you see.
They complain about their day,
And wish their parents away.

As a young carer, emotions are hard,
Anger, resentment and sadness are barred.
That is because a little voice said,
'You're a parent to a parent, don't lose your head.'

As a young carer, I have learnt life skills,
I can cook, clean and I can pay bills.
But if my emotions go to town,
Then I have music to calm me down.

Rebecca Harris (13)
Fowey River Academy, Fowey

3000

What will the year 3000 be?
Will we live in the sky or under the sea?
Will there be aliens from outer space?
And will Facebook have its own face?

Can DeLoreans finally time travel?
And can sleeping bags self-unravel?
Can penguins fly?
And can robots cry?

I wonder what year 3000 will hold?
All I know is I'll be very old,
I hope global warming will amend,
Or least the world doesn't end.

Ben Jordan (14)
Fowey River Academy, Fowey

UNTITLED

She's a growing force inside me
Just waiting to tear out
Every day I ask her to leave
But she's staying, there's no doubt.

She stops me answering questions
She makes me tell them 'I'm alright'
But really she's exposing my private thoughts
And my tears flow like a river at night.

She used to be a small part of me
However now she freely roams
Ripping out my heartstrings
Until the only feeling I possess is alone.

I can't remember being myself
When my friends and I could relate
But now I'm hiding in her shadow
And I'm struggling to escape.

Lauren James (14)
Fowey River Academy, Fowey

AT SCHOOL

Waiting to die at school
Wish I could fly at school
Never look at the sky at school
Not going to survive at school
It's going to kill me
Not going to thrill me
It might give me scars
Or lock me up behind bars
This is the last paper I will own
Also they will lock me up
And take my cell phone
That is basically life at school.

Ben Congerton (13)
Fowey River Academy, Fowey

MY FUTURE

My future is a question mark
Now I feel I'm in the dark
There's so much I want to do
But right now I don't have a clue

Beautician, lawyer, singer, dancer
I just don't know, what is the answer?
What on earth will I become?
Will I get married and be a mum?

Will I meet a handsome man?
My very own Superman!
Will I be rich or will I be poor?
Will I be good or break the law?

Will I own a lot of land
And own a house that's really grand?
My future is a question mark
Right now I feel I'm in the dark.

Helen Sophie Rowan (11)
Fowey River Academy, Fowey

MY DAD

It's in my head, it's there to stay
It's a game I'm losing every day
I look at him and I think
You let my mum's heart go down the sink
I remember the year, day and even the time
Even the minute I heard the wedding bells chime
Six years later you come running back
You said you can't do this, you said she's like an addictive snack
You told her you love and need her
And that without her your life's a blur
Now you've got the privilege to marry my mum
And Dad . . . you're way more lucky than some.

Carla Jacobs (14)
Fowey River Academy, Fowey

THE FUTURE

The flames of factories glow,
The flying cars flow,
No trees will ever grow;
And no one will know.

The iPhone 6 is old,
The new one's made of gold,
The best ever car was a Mini,
But it vanished like Houdini.

ISIS are a threat,
But we will never forget,
What they did in Paris,
Making the world feel harassed.

The future scares me,
Global warming and weaponry,
Advancing technology,
Could leave the world in jeopardy.

Ross Jezard (13)
Fowey River Academy, Fowey

IF I WERE A SUPERHERO!

If I were a superhero,
I'd be big and strong.

Super fast and super smart,
with a super song.

Saving people,
all day long.

With a smile,
on my face.

Flying overhead,
keeping everybody safe.

Alfie Commander (11)
Fowey River Academy, Fowey

LACK OF POETIC SKILL

I need to write a poem,
It has to be quite long,
I can't think of the right words,
It's all just going wrong.

I really cannot do it,
I'm running out of time,
And what stops me in my tracks is,
That this all has to rhyme.

I can do equations,
Science and French as well,
Even drawing complex artwork,
But poems are just hell!

I simply cannot do this
I must just accept my fate
I could never write a poem,
Oh . . . hang on, wait . . .

Samuel Silburn (12)
Fowey River Academy, Fowey

MY EMOTIONS

When I feel sad,
I feel grey and blue

When I feel excited,
My heart beats like a rapid cheetah

When I feel lonely,
I feel like an old odd sock

When I feel challenged
I feel stuck in a pit

When I feel happy
I feel like a field of flowers, soaking up the sun.

James Lake (12)
Fowey River Academy, Fowey

ACME

Muscle-tearing climb, exhaustion in my legs,
It was like hell under my coat, sweat dripping from my body,
The only sound I hear is the crunching of snow and the violent exhaling of others around me,
Step after hellish step, slowly progressing but it seems no closer,
Devilish boots underfoot seem to be clawing into my feet,
Ever-growing weight of skis on my back,
I feel the sun pushing down on top of me, crushing me with its intense heat,
I'm focused on one thing: reaching the top.
As I finally summit, I collapse onto the soft, cool snow, inhaling deeply,
I can feel a satisfying breeze on my face,
I muster the strength to stand, gear up and descend,
The mountains a blur in my vision,
I feel a sense of danger around me,
Going faster, faster, faster, until I'm there . . .

Tristan Reed (15)
Fowey River Academy, Fowey

BULLIES

We're all unique
Whether we're a geek or a freak
We all need to speak
Just because we're different doesn't mean one of us is weak
Whether we're fat, whether we're thin
Who cares about the colour of our skin
We're all in this together, we will all succeed and win
Let's let out our feelings we have within
We're all the same
None of us lame
This is not a game
Stop with the bullies
Stand up!

Libby Patton (11)
Fowey River Academy, Fowey

THE FUTURE

If you yearn for the illusion of freedom, prepare for the unethical end,
Exploited countries begin to descend,
It's only when it begins to perish,
You realise what you truly cherish,
Not even all the riches in the land,
Are worth this isolated, obscene world of sand,
Radicals, rebels, outcasts and pioneers rise from the debris and ash,
As societies' opinions clash,
You said let liberty, independence and equality commence,
But you never said at what expense,
Sugar-coated fantasies slip from your grasp,
Breathe,
This is your last chance,
I may have revived you from this livid abyss,
But I leave these forlorn relics, now immersed in green,
To remind our oppressed humanity, not to dream.

Elisha Murphy (13)
Fowey River Academy, Fowey

FUTURE

Young children dreaming about the future.
What they could be dreaming.
Technology, family or even being famous.
What sort of person will they be?
Dreaming about the future.
What job they're going to have.
In the future where they live.
Dreaming 'I want to be an astronaut'.
Are these dreams possible?
Adults, do they dream
Dream about who they are going to be?
Questions: what does the future mean to different people?
Are futures and dreams possible?

Leah Saint (14)
Fowey River Academy, Fowey

YOU AND ME

My heart was thumping
I stood there in awe

The butterflies were out
Freely once more

Your handsome face
Made me look a disgrace

As your eyes glistened
I looked at you and listened

You and me make a perfect match
Can't you just see we're perfectly attached

My one and only
Through the bad and the good

Although the whole thing
Is totally misunderstood!

Kymberley Snell (11)
Fowey River Academy, Fowey

LOVE IS MADE TO LAST

I think of you as a sister
I think of you as a listener

For all those times we've laughed
All those memories handcrafted
Perfect memories photographed

You are my first and last
Once-in-a-lifetime friend
Because love is made to last

You are my best friend, no doubt
Included,
You make rivers flow from my
Eyes, crying excluded.

Issy Rhodes (12)
Fowey River Academy, Fowey

WORDS

I don't know
what words to write
to put on paper, some
stranger's choice of theme

And I don't feel enough
to bleed it, onto the paper
so blank and white. For
everyone to read my truth laid bare
in solid words of Biro blue ink

I may lapse, or not love. Every
yesterday that could've been
But it will not be drawn through
this poem. In a place so public and
harsh, where my solid words
melt molten and unapproachable

Silvered thoughts strung together, glinting
like fish in the blue under a maybe sky
hidden by changing waters
Not to be heard above another's lyrics
Behind a wall of clouds. 'Wondering who I copy.'

Cora Cooper (15)
Fowey River Academy, Fowey

SEEING RED

Red is familiar,
Shapes and patterns,
Thick, thin,
I see red.

Never the same, never different,
But pinches like the cold on blue fingers,
Sharp like electric,
The red is never gone.

Seeps through minds,
Stains like mud,
Purposefully,
Or not.

It brings silent joy for those who stay,
But a constant bygone for those who are stuck here.
Red sees me.

Elise Wood (14)
Fowey River Academy, Fowey

THE DARK WALK

Wondering through the streets
She sighed with regret
Thinking what the day would be like next

Her footsteps silent on the damp, gloomy floor
Her tears encasing her face as she walked on and on . . .

For she had nowhere to be
Nothing to do
Nothing to say . . .

All of a sudden
She ground to a halt
As she glared into the murky puddles beyond

Her mind was riddled with thoughts
Her head in overload
She was thinking about something that should never be heard . . .

Isabel Wolf (12)
Fowey River Academy, Fowey

THE WAVE

The wave goes smash
The surfers go crash
As far as the eye can see

And I will be as happy as can be
Because I am with my gang
And when it will be the perfect day for me
Then my life shall go off with a bang

I will stand on my toes
Or stand on one knee
But I don't care when I'm in the sea

Because the perfect day for me
Will be when I am free
And I'm with all my friends at sea.

Joseph Wharton (11)
Fowey River Academy, Fowey

THE FUTURE

Wish we could turn back time,
To the good old days,
When the mind was free,
And the fears at bay.

Life goes on too fast,
Yet time ceases to pass,
Younger children seem so free,
Older people far from glee.

Time is a predator,
Preying on the weak,
Waiting for the good times,
To come along and eat.

I wonder what my future holds,
Whatever it is, I'm sure it'll be gold.

Harry Phillips (14)
Fowey River Academy, Fowey

ANGER

Anger, a stream of lava rushing past rocks
The evil ticks and tocks of clocks
As anger takes over your mind
The one emotion that takes over mankind
Lock your doors but lock them tight
Anger patrols the streets tonight.

Anger is just a flame, put out day after day
Put up a fight and edge it away
The more it builds up inside you
The easier it will be to burst out at others.

Anger cannot be continued forever
Don't let it bundle up inside like stormy weather
Joy can overthrow it, just wait, you'll see
It can bring your sunken boat back to the surface of the sea.

Chloe Roach (11)
Fowey River Academy, Fowey

POEM ABOUT ROWING

I listen for the continuous clashing of six oars and pins to keep in time
I can hear the swoosh of the water as I heave my oar through the whistling waves
The coxswain shouts again and the pressure, power and pace goes up for twenty strokes,
All the moored up boats beside us, bob forwards, backwards, up and down like circus animals
I can see clouds of my warm breath as it enters the icy air
Ripples form on the surface and cold water runs down my skin as the dread of rain enters our minds
I'm exhausted, freezing cold and soaking wet
My muscles ache, my feet are numb and my hands are sore from blisters
As the boat scrapes against the rocky shore of Fowey, we relax as that's our training session over.

Jasmine George (12)
Fowey River Academy, Fowey

UNTITLED

Earth is 4.5 billion years old.
Mankind?
About 140,000.
In perspective, if the Earth's lifespan was 24 hours,
We've been here for . . .
. . . three seconds.
We have led animals to extinction over a 1,000 times the normal rate.
Lions, rhinos, elephants, tigers, leopards,
Gone,
Gone in just three seconds.
There are animals that have been here longer than us.
Humans named themselves 'homo sapiens',
Latin for 'wise man'.
Extinction is not wise.

Liam Barron (13)
Fowey River Academy, Fowey

HOCKEY SUCCESS

On the pitch, waiting for pushback,
We all stare at centre forward, waiting for that ball to be hit,
Suddenly, you hear the vibrations off the sticks as the ball bounces into it,
From white to black, from pink to blue,
The gum shields are not removed,
Half-time arrives with open wounds with blood trickling down,
Tough, tough ladies with no frowns,
The smell of fresh air with a hint of the bitter brewery,
The blood, the adrenaline, pumping through our veins, when second half starts,
It's time for the ball, hitting the back board quickly,
Victorious screams, defeated tears,
Time to go out to celebrate with beers.

Jess Gough (14)
Fowey River Academy, Fowey

MY DREAMS

My dreams for the future are . . .
No wars
No hate
A world where everyone lives in peace.
Where you are respected by everyone
and the police are never needed.
A world without pain
or illness
or suffering.
A world without sadness
just lots of happiness.
A world filled with smiley people.
I can dream.
Can't I?

Rory Winch (12)
Fowey River Academy, Fowey

TEENAGE TURMOIL

They say teenage years are time to treasure,
But for most it's a period of pressure.
We're all teens for better or for worse,
But is this a blessing or is it a curse?
The pretty girl's popular because of her looks,
Whilst the only friends the 'nerd' has are the ones in her books.
You have to be skinny is taught by the press,
But shouldn't we focus on the results of our tests?
Every time I've turned on the TV,
Air-brushed models are all that I see.
When it comes to love, we're too young to know what we want,
But we're already meant to decide our future jobs.
And whilst all these words are true,
At the end of the day, your future's down to you.

Millie Grose (12)
Fowey River Academy, Fowey

PLANET PURIFICATION

Powders ploughing through the sky.
Is this what the future could be?
Zombies snarling, fleeing, charging.
Is this what the future could be?
Who will know what the future could be?
All we know is it's coming.
Rocks and mountains and rumbling seas.
Men with no fingers, toes or knees.
Six planets left in the galaxy.
Is this what the future could be?
Or it could be all our dreams.
No pollution or to be fear free.
But there's no need to worry for now
The future is far from here.

Tyler Alan Morcom (11)
Fowey River Academy, Fowey

TODAY IS MY TOMORROW'S YESTERDAY

So wake up to yet another sleep
One whose fingers prance around the necks
And when you least expect it to, it sits
And waits

Oh child! Don't be fooled
As these shadows are made by you
If you let them move away slow
Light will show

Come forth oh whispers of treachery
Those that put tomorrow behind me
Saying words of betrayal and heartbreak
But when I challenge to a duel, turn into smiles in happy lakes

I take an oath by you, those who seek my yesterday
Don't hold back your power for the demons in your mind
As you have a sword so fierce in might
Don't hold it back, remember to fight

This powerful tool not many observe
It comes to you without a fee
Built up by friendship, family and kindness' fence
But the grip is none but common sense

The dreams it shatters as if glass
Because you don't have a grip made of that
So let yourself forward from the dreams you can't let go
Because every step you take is one step more

These angels in disguise come to knock on your door
They look you in the eye
But you stare back
This time again certainty is what you lack

So when support comes to kiss your feet
Let the fragrance of heaven flood your home
As the key to the thought
That today is my tomorrow's yesterday has arrived.

Maryam Bibi Sidat (14)
Islamiyah Girls' High School, Blackburn

MINDLESS WISDOM

The Internet is as sharp as a knife
Wasting our entire life
Why are you still in doubt?
Your time is running out . . .
Is it not your duty
To enjoy the world's beauty?

Gadgets, widgets and games
Are not giving you fame
They're really pushing you towards shame
And making you lame . . .
Why on earth don't we care
About what's happening out there?

We're trying to beat our high score
Yet we don't know those next door
We're so obsessed with this
And all the things we miss
All the beauty and bliss
Why are we doing this?

From our jobs we get fired
And yet we're still not tired
It's so pretty out there
And we don't even care

Our parents are trying to say
Don't waste your time in play
You're wasting the entire day
You're walking towards dismay
And yet you shout hooray!
I don't need to pay!

Twitter, Insta and Snapchat
Are making us fat
Covering us in their hat
And then throwing us on a mat

Tumblr, YouTube and Facebook
Are telling us not to look
Like just eat don't cook
That family members suck

But are we in luck?
We're just covered in muck!

So listen to me now
Without saying how
We need to change quick
Before we stick

To the gadgets out there
Without any flair
So let's not glare
Or even stare
And let's be aware
And care.

Ubab Malik (11)
Islamiyah Girls' High School, Blackburn

HOWLING WIND

The wind howls like a hungry fox,
Waiting for its predator, a ticking clock,
Out every day, morning and night,
Everywhere you look always in sight.

The wind howls like violent pain,
Aching and aching it won't go away,
Out every day, morning and night,
Everywhere you look always in sight.

The wind howls like spirals of air,
Whispering in your ear it'll always be there,
Out every day, morning and night,
Everywhere you look always in sight.

The wind howls gently through the night,
Passing by giving people a fright,
Out every day, morning and night,
Everywhere you look always in sight.

Howling wind, howling wind.

Nazifa Rahman (12)
Islamiyah Girls' High School, Blackburn

WINTER WONDERLAND

Winter is cold
The wind so fierce and bold
There is ice in the sky
I think I am going to slip, 'Oh my!'
The squirrel gathers nuts
It doesn't even need a hut
And the wild geese fly
All of them passing by
The fluffy red fox
taking shelter in a box.

Has his fur to keep him warm
from the swarm,
of flying snowflakes
The bear in her cave
Trying to be brave
and sleeping through the storm
as the snow outside begins to form.

Now while all this is going on
A little boy in his room tries to look upon
all the wondrous things
the swans' with their flowing, graceful wings
illuminating the moonlight, trying to catch sight
of the snow-white fur
of the exquisite white rabbit
searching for the place where it inhabits

Suddenly! The door bursts open
Mum rushes in! Hurry, hurry, hide under the covers
before she discovers
what you have been up to
doing the things that you aren't meant to do
that you have been awake
and trying to fake
your sleep
like a terrified sheep.

The door shuts
'Phew,' that was close
I think I bumped my nose

in all the commotion
I might need some lotion
Now it's time to go to sleep
slowly counting sheep
eyes drifting into a trance
Hey! That rhymes with France!
To have dreams about,
beautiful boxes and busy squirrels,
about big bears and rushing rabbits,
gradually heading into a winter wonderland.

Haneefa Bhatti (13)
Islamiyah Girls' High School, Blackburn

THE GEMS IN MY HEART

My mum is someone very rare
Because for me she always seems to care
She always makes my day
Without her my life would be grey
Daily she makes my food
And puts me in a good mood
My dad is a sweet soft bear
Another person who is very rare
He is so comforting
Though he can't talk English he still tries to keep up with the bling
I love him very much
A person with characteristics like him there is no such
My parents are both very kind
People as caring as them you'll never be able to find
I have the best mum and dad
They still love me even though I drive them mad
In my life they play a big part
The reason they'll always have a place in my heart.

Umaiyyah Choudhury (13)
Islamiyah Girls' High School, Blackburn

A LETTER TO THE FOE, DEPRESSION

Dear Depression.
My devotion and duty was never lost towards you.
I crashed on affliction's waves like a lost boat.
I was drowning with the thought that I was lost in a bottomless pit of no hope.
You, Depression, combed my mouth into a house of heavy hesitation but you
had the audacity to name it a vacant wilderness.
Day after wretched day.
You would take me by the hand.
Your razor blade fingers digging deep into my skin as you dragged along.
So, I grew up thinking no one would love me.
Loving you got me sick.
Got me suicide-watched.
Got me cutting.
Got me depressed enough to be named the 'miserable child'.
I couldn't go outside, because outside was where my fears had settled.
I had to practise staying as still as a summer noon.
I had to practise staying as silent as death.
You, Depression, were my foe.
You always told me what to do.
You were my lover.
I would tell you I couldn't do this anymore.
That I felt like my heart had holes that would never be filled.
That a tied rope would love me more than anyone ever did.
But now I want to tell you that I am letting go.
I am letting go of you.
And I know that I can drop that blade.
I will not cease.
I will not be silenced, because me and you, shall forever be strangers now.

Saffa Naeem (12)
Islamiyah Girls' High School, Blackburn

NO ESCAPE

As I sit there, a tear trickling down my face
Every second, minute, hour, day, month, year
My parents arguing, shouting, screaming
A tear trickling down my face
I go to school to escape the horror
It's not different there
Bullying, that's the matter
I'm different, so what?
A tear trickling down my face
I sit there staring into space
Hearing the teacher drone on and on
Dring, dring, dring
The sound of escape!
As I walk home, kicking stones
A tear trickling down my face
I want to open up, burst like a volcano
But who to tell?
No friends, no one there for me
I go home, Mum's sitting there
Staring into space, 'Mum, where's Dad?'
A tear trickling down her face
She says sorry, I answer, 'For what?'
She says, 'Father's gone.' I go to comfort her
She pushes me away, I fall, I bang my head
Blood trickling down my face
I walk out the door, run, keep on running
Car . . . *Beep!*
I see black, then a white light
A bright white light
Last thing I remember, my mum beat me.

Salma Ibrahim Sidat (11)
Islamiyah Girls' High School, Blackburn

DEPRESSION! – THE KILLER

Depression is a fight
A fight till death
Every word is a stab
Every thought is always sad
Every action is a wound
A wound on yourself
Depression is a corpse
You are the walking dead
You are unaware but still alive
Stare out the window like a rejected, broken doll
Depression is a very bad dream
You are never going to wake up
Always darkness in your eyes
No light shines from above, you tell everyone lies
You're helpless and insane
Depression is an ocean of emotions
Only sadness stands tall in your way
Emptiness kills your heart
A growling storm awaits
Which you're never going to face
You try to avoid it but it just lures you in like a demon
The waves crash against your head
Screaming and crying
You try hard to keep it in
But one day it won't last
There will be help someday
That day will be when nothing stands in your *way!*

Safiyyah Haider (11)
Islamiyah Girls' High School, Blackburn

WINTER WONDERLAND

Crunching footsteps on the ground,
falling snowflakes all around,
winter winds howling due to the storm,
a thick white blanket covering the lawn,
catching snowflakes on your tongue,
enjoying the snow all day long,
children building carrot-nosed snowmen,
we all know winter will come again!

Seeing your breath escape into the mist,
scribbling down your Christmas wish list,
setting down cookies on a plate,
isn't it agony just to wait,
for Christmas Day to come at last?
Sharing memories from the past,
babies, children, ladies and men,
we all know winter will come again!

Flying with his reindeer in the sky,
Santa soars through the night,
leaving presents under the tree,
leaving them all for you and me,
then climbing back up the chimney,
and we wake up lit up with glee,
Santa flies back to his den,
we all know winter will come again!

Maliha Ali (12)
Islamiyah Girls' High School, Blackburn

MUSIC!

Music is like a cool winter breeze that picks you up and takes you to another world.
When music is being played everything that is lovely grows even lovelier.
The melody of music is like a huge scoop of your favourite type of ice cream.
It clears and empties your mind telling you to lay back and enjoy the beat.
Life without music is like a flower without petals.
Life without music is like a bed without a blanket.
Life without music is like a book without a story.
Music goes with anything, just like chips go with ketchup.
Music has a meaning of expressing yourself the way you dress, the things you eat and the words you say.
Music lets your feelings come alive.
It lets you move, sing and shout.
Without it our souls would have no rhythm . . .

Aqsa Wajid (11)
Islamiyah Girls' High School, Blackburn

LONELINESS

A room with no windows or doors,
A trapped soul in a box,
A sheep lost from its herd,
A deserted island,
A black hole,
A feeling of despair,
An overcast sky,
No one to cherish my love with but myself,
A piercing scream.

Maria Jiva (12)
Islamiyah Girls' High School, Blackburn

THE FORGETTING SOUL

The fire of emotion, the nucleus of one's existence.
Electric network of a hundred billion cells.
Experiences imprisoned into forgotten memory.
Just floating clouds of white matter that once defined identity.
Confined in a concave cavity, pitched into dark silence inside,
Though cognisant of lights illuminating, and bells ringing in from outside.
Once the blissful soul of mind, of heart and body,
In delicate imbalance – it extinguishes, diminishes and mortifies.
Kith and kin and those aware, frantically despair,
The loss of the forgetting soul, often too much to bear.
Erased memories, stripped of dignity.
Life paces slow as the end beckons to infinity.
Yet pain is still felt, and shrieks of cries and tears are shed.
The heart still beats, yearning love from those who cared,
To believe in the soul of souls that resides within,
This graceful presence, so rejoice, come in.

Zaynab Maria Amin (12)
Islamiyah Girls' High School, Blackburn

'MORE'

It's more than being crazy, being crackers,
Being lazy, being slackers, skiving school
Or benefits. It's more than being down
Or 'just a little blue', more then being
Sad sometimes; it's being helpless and
Not knowing what to do.

It's being scared and anxious,
Utterly depressed or getting stressed and it's
Not having motivation to get up or
To get dressed; surely this day will be
As lousy as the last? Every day's a struggle
To not be haunted by the past.

It's not managing to sleep and
Dozing through the day, and it's
Struggling to keep food down as guilt
Eats you away – it's contemplating life
And whether it's worthwhile, and hoping
No one notices the sadness in your smile.

It's watching angry redness as
It sears across your skin and
Praying nobody can see the pain you keep within.
It's self-hatred, it's compulsion and sleep-depriving fear,
Mental illnesses are brutal and hurt
Millions every year.

Megan Elizabeth Thomas (17)
Liverpool College, Liverpool

SIMPLY CARRY ON

It is very simple to leave something
Behind when your heart is a big and
Empty void that swallows every
Emotion a person could feel.

It is very easy to look back on your
Life and forget what suddenly
Stained your whole existence; while
Asking yourself, *where did I go wrong?*

It is very effortless to push away
Every single one of your problems while your
Already weak voice tries to reach out for
Someone – anyone – who remembers how to love!

To think that nothing you do is
Accepted by society no matter how much you
Try to fit in and prove that you are worthy of a place in this
Frost-coated world. And all you want to do is just give up.

When that happens, just close your eyes and
Let the winter snow carry your struggles
Away like old and dry leaves
Tumbling across the sidewalk.

Then: stand tall and start over.
Keep trying against all the
Odds that may never be
In your favour.

Even if the reality burns and
You are the only one who doesn't panic.

Milena Milica Matvejeva (15)
Lodge Park Academy, Corby

2020 EVACUATION

The airport was in chaos,
Parents and children alike rushing to the aeroplane;
My mother and I included
I thought back to this morning;
Breakfast, bath, brushed hair,
All normalities in other days.
But this was no normal day . . .
I was being sent off,
Or so Mother says.
She says it's for my safety,
To keep me from the war.
I choked back tears for I must be brave,
My ribs aching from the crying I'd already done.
Like the soldiers I marched on;
Head held high as royalty does.
'All aboard!' the pilot ordered.
'Be strong,' Mother said;
Her eyes spilling water.
Behind her tears I could see,
A mother's pride held for me,
With a last farewell I took my seat
Not knowing that mother and child . . .
Will never again meet.

Chloe Jessica McMaster (15)
Lodge Park Academy, Corby

CHANGE

The idea of what is one day may not be another
May scare one,
But truly, everything is scary, every sister and every brother,
Everything changes under the sun,
But someday you'll get over this,
And then you'll be in true bliss.

Jessica Dance (15)
Lodge Park Academy, Corby

MY FATHER'S ENDING

I lost my father one day.
His skull still perched in my room.
What an impressive sight it is.
The fungus, mould, brown like dry blood.
I did shed teardrops on this day . . .
Happiness!

My father's phantom eyes stay in his skull.
If you compress them they tremble,
Such a pleasant thought.
They are my most delightful treasure.
Looking at it with no worry, feeling alive,
Free!

I have no sorrow towards my father,
The way he treated me.
The dried-up scars and discoloured marks
To prove the monster I lived with
My target has now been met,
Bullseye!

Ellie Thain (16)
Lodge Park Academy, Corby

FUTURE

I feel the cool breeze
As I stand on sad height
These tall buildings built to please
Block out all sunlight.

A warning to us on pity
By the man upstairs
I wander the streets of New York City
Looking for someone in this world who cares.

Our society weak,
So our future is bleak.

Drew Thoirs (15)
Lodge Park Academy, Corby

SHE KNOWS

It's like Groundhog Day
It's the same routine every single night

6 o'clock comes, she runs to her room
And hides,
She tries to imagine a world where
She will never feel so scared and useless

Her mother's scream pierces through her
Thoughts, and travels through her spine

It's begun

She hears the force of his punches,
She feels sick, how

Can a man do that to a woman
He once loved, how can he do
That seeing the terror in her eyes?

Verbal venom oozes out his mouth

She knows.

She knows at this very moment her
Mother is struggling for her life and
All she can do is hide.

Storm-Elisha Milne (15)
Lodge Park Academy, Corby

HAVE YOU HEARD THE MOUNTAINS WHISPER?

She travels alone on a long
Winding road, dipping in and out
Between the dusky mountains, strong
With the whispers of the wind's sweet shout.
Her nightmare has been reduced
To just a daily struggle, a mistake,
A fight, she left confused . . .
Staying would mean she would retake
The care that she once had, not again. What a mistake.

A bundle of possessions slung across
Her back, she walks, walks, just keeps going.
The pain of leaving is nothing, she is used to loss,
Affectionate to sweet, sensitive souls, suffering keeps growing.
Like the royal blue skies pulling up above
She will draw back to being bright
But for now she is settled, the isolation fits like a glove
Until she finds a new home and stops as peaceful
As a dove

So she travels alone, on a long winding road . . .

Rebecca Bell (16)
Lodge Park Academy, Corby

'THEY' USED TO BE 'US'

Shudders ripple through the classroom,
Tiny waves of sympathetic murmurs and angry words.
They are young, and better off for it.
A list of names on the wall, too many to count.
They loved too loudly, their killers had said, existed too proudly.
Teacher's face has aged a hundred years, old pain becoming
Fresh again in her eyes.
Her fears have been put to rest now,
People know, but are unaffected.
She does not feel unsafe.

'This is our history.
Our race has made mistakes.
But don't worry, children, there's no danger here.
You're safe now.
To love, and laugh, and have no fear.'
The small ones sigh, then start to smile.
It's been this way now for a while.
If you still live in the past, take heed,
And wash out the hate for which
There is no need.

Eleanor King (15)
Lodge Park Academy, Corby

THE MAN

He who lays alone
Separated from the outside world
Pictures his past life

A world with society, normal clothes
Education and equality
A place where communication is a virtue
Rather than a beating

A quick glance or a signal of little understanding
A region where he and his people used to belong
Before a five-pointed star showed evil
Where no evil was present

Now he lays as a young man
Singled out by his fellow men
His fate is soon upon him
As the rain beats down and the colouring
On his striped pyjamas oozes out
To join the men, women and children he used to know.

Luke Joseph Starrs (15)
Lodge Park Academy, Corby

HER

Hundreds of sickening memories running through
Her mind, possessions in which
She takes forever

Yet she stays.

Closed eyes. Broken smiles. Stuck in
The torturous clutches of love
Unable to forget . . .

Yet she stays.

Blackened. Bruised. Beaten
She remained in love with the
One thing that has taken away her soul

Yet she stays.

Iara Alves (15)
Lodge Park Academy, Corby

DOWNHILL THRILL

Adrenaline pumping, heart racing,
Hands shaking, eyeing up the first turn,
The gate drops
And before I know it I am at the berm,
The speed is unreal,
Over the table top,
It gives me such a thrill,
Faster, faster here I go,
Before I know it, I hit a bump,
I've started to pick up a good flow,
The finish line is in sight,
There is the last jump,
Pedal, pedal, pedal to get some height,
The tracks got thinner,
I've crossed the line,
Am I the winner?

Josh Ford (11)
Maidenhill School, Stonehouse

DESTINY

Unaware of the people around me,
Lost in my own dead world,
Scared of the things that I don't know,
Trapped in a cage, all alone.

Just trying to survive each day,
Lost and afraid,
Beginning to fade,
I just don't belong.

I try to run away from the fear and hatred,
But it keeps catching me up,
Swallowing me whole,
Tearing away at my soul.

Blending in with the crowd,
I lose my true inner self,
My heart is failing,
Self-confidence disappearing in the storm.

I'm not going to be held down any longer,
I want to be free to explore and wander,
To experience the beauty that life has to offer.

My body slowly comes to life,
A fresh start, a new beginning,
Freedom unleashes me into the wild,
This is my chance.

I leap and twirl,
I'm finally free,
I sing and laugh,
It's good to be me.

Maybe life isn't so bad,
I just need to step out of the shadows
And make my own destiny.

Alicia Salmon (12)
Maidenhill School, Stonehouse

MY FIRST TOURNAMENT

I stepped in line to grab the right javelin for me.
I had mixed emotions.
I didn't know what to feel.
Just then I found myself seconds before my go.
I didn't want to do it.
I haven't been here before, how could I possibly throw?
The sky was pink.
All I could hear was my heart beating.
It was breathtaking.
I was shocked with how far other people threw,
It was significant.
I felt a little tap on my shoulder,
It was my coach and sister.
We had a pep talk.
I was number 78.
They called my number.
The thing with throwing a javelin is
That it's like a maths sum,
You have to remember all the tricky steps.
I did the run-up then stopped,
My coach said I could have another go later on.
I failed first go,
I felt embarrassed.
Why though, I was way younger than the rest.
I sat on the bar filled with amazement,
Thinking, *could I ever win?*
Well I guess we have to wait for the future.

Reece Shipway-Squibb (12)
Maidenhill School, Stonehouse

MY LIFE

When I wake up in the morning
Ideas pop into my head
Will I do something exciting?
Or I could just laze in bed.

I could play on my iPad
Or take a long hot bath.
Perhaps I'll meet up with my mates
And we'll go out and have a laugh.

Because laughter is important
Happiness is too,
I always try to wear a smile
In everything I do.

So maybe it's gymnastics
Or riding on your bike,
Try to spend some time each day
Doing something that you like.

Try to follow your hopes and dreams
And make the most of every day.
Don't waste your time by feeling bored
That's really not the way.

So get yourself up early
Make the most of your whole day
You must live, love and be happy
That's what I'd like to say.

Mia Bennett (11)
Maidenhill School, Stonehouse

A DAY IN THE LIFE OF A FOX

The sun's gone down, the moon is bright,
It's time to play because it's night.
I've left the den dance through the fields,
I'm off to the city to find a meal.

My coat is red and shines bright,
As I trot along in the moonlight.
I find a road, now this is a task,
I'm scared as I dodge the cars so fast.

I have to hide in the bush,
Especially when the big cars whoosh!
I know nobody can see me here
But I'm still scared shaking with fear.

I've found some cat food down a lane,
I think I'll come back here again.
I'm by the road, I'm really scared,
Quick, there are no cars, I'm prepared.

I bolt through the fields lightning-fast,
I'm back with my mate and cubs at last.
I lay the food down on the floor,
My cubs were hungry, not anymore.

I love where I live,
Things can be new,
But most, I love my mate
And our cubs too.

Ellie Gardiner (12)
Maidenhill School, Stonehouse

THE FUTURE

The future can be exciting,
Sad or happy, we cannot tell,
Sometimes scary when we think about it,
But it usually turns out well.

Tomorrow's world is up to us,
We must look after what's ours,
Reduce, reuse, recycle,
Cut pollution from factories, rubbish and cars.

Technology has changed the world,
In many different ways,
We can quickly look up information,
Which would have taken days.

Scientists are working hard,
To help those who are ill,
So let's hope that in the future,
They find a cure with a pill.

The future comes so fast,
Unseen but always there,
Always just in front of us,
Waiting for us all to share.

Our past we can't go back to,
It has been and it has gone,
Yesterday is just a memory,
To think of when days are long.

Charlotte Cook (12)
Maidenhill School, Stonehouse

MY ACHIEVEMENT

Homework is done, time to get in the car,
A quick snack eaten, good job gym's not far.
Leotard and shorts all packed in my bag,
Time to get changed, I guess gym's not that bad.
I walk through the door, my friends are all there,
Warm-up just starting, I should be over there!
I need to get changed – quick let's hurry,
No time to waste before I start to worry.
My coach will be shouting if I am late,
I really don't want to make any mistakes.
My coach has decided to try a new trick tonight,
Don't want to do it but must be polite.
Let's try it and see if I can get to the end,
That track seems so long but will fight to the end.
My friends all cheering, my mum is so proud,
Let's do it, it sounds like an amazing crowd.
My heart is pounding, my hands start to shake,
I am so scared right now, everything aches.
I am next on the track, let's do my best,
I hope I achieve this, however I am stressed.
I run and I flip, I twist and I whip,
My only fear is I hope I don't trip.
Well I did it! Enjoyed it! It was hard work and fun,
My goal has been achieved and a gold medal won.
The hard work and training, long hours and pain
Have fulfilled my dream and a gymnast I became.

Beth Roberts (12)
Maidenhill School, Stonehouse

THE END OF THE WORLD HAS JUST BEGUN

The end of the world has just begun,
Along with the stars, the moon and the sun.
Everything is crumbling like my tummy is rumbling.
People are scared and are not prepared,
With volcanoes erupting, with villains corrupting,
Time is running out, of that we have no doubt.
People are scared and worried
And unhappy about what it would do to us as a family.
I won't see my children grow
Which is just not fair,
Just thinking about it is too hard to bear.
All around are people crying
With sad memories of people dying
So don't just stand there and wait,
Live your life before it is too late.
All around the world is great
From every day to every date.
The world will always be ours
Even though it won't be here for 24 hours.
So before your time has run out
Make sure you smile, not pout
To show you're happy not scared
To make your friends and yourself be prepared
For what's ahead of your journey.

Isobelle Lily Elizabeth Herbert (11)
Maidenhill School, Stonehouse

MY SOMEONE SPECIAL

I'm thinking of someone special,
Who means the world to me,
But my someone special has a secret,
Something not everyone can see,
Inside he fights an illness,
That makes every day more tough,
We try to make the most of time,
But will we have enough?
He still shows the world his smile,
Doesn't let it get him down,
Wants to make the most of every moment,
Not sit around and frown,
In some ways we are grateful,
We get our second chance,
To make a thousand more memories,
It could have been a worse circumstance,
I'll miss his funny laughter,
I'll really miss his smile,
I'll miss the way he hugs me
And goes the extra mile,
But right now we're still together
And I hope it stays that way,
We will never give up hope,
They will find a way to help him stay.

Alesha Katie Barker (12)
Maidenhill School, Stonehouse

ABANDONED BY WAR

Enjoying the warm weather,
Nothing could go wrong,
With the sun beaming on you
And the boats in the distance,
In a beautiful city,
Peace and happiness . . .
Not for long.

Storming boats from the shore,
Armed men running, calling,
Explosions everywhere,
Seems like nowhere to go,
Fleeing, screaming, unbearable to watch,
How could it happen?
Innocent civilians falling.

Once populated, now deserted,
A desolate, eerie place,
Haunting echoes long forgotten,
No chance of going back,
Will this tragic event leave our minds?
Remembering the pain,
A once known city, no trace.

Tom Organ (11)
Maidenhill School, Stonehouse

BULLYING

People who bully are so shallow
They try to make you feel worthless and hollow
People who kick are so thick
People who are mad make you feel sad
People who say words make you feel worse
People who are spiteful find it delightful
People who hate make you be late
People who are dumb make you feel glum.

Phoenix Masson-Day (12)
Maidenhill School, Stonehouse

THE CONSEQUENCE OF DEATH

He comes knocking on your door,
You know your life's not right,
He has those eyes of murder
And he's something you can't fight.

First you hear the scraping sound,
Running through your head,
Then you hear a screaming sound,
You realise you are dead.

As you're falling through the earth
Your heart starts beating fast,
The question on your lips
Is, 'Am I good or am I bad?'

If you're good, then to Heaven you go,
A place of luxury,
If you're bad, then oh no,
Hell's no place to rest in peace.

My message to you now,
Before you cartwheel to death's door,
Be good 'cause you know why,
'Cause Hell's not right at all.

Molly Riddell (12)
Maidenhill School, Stonehouse

BE UNIQUE

B eing unique is fun,
E specially if you're the only one,

U nderstanding yourself, it's fine,
N o one else is like you,
I know it might sound fine,
Q uiet, can you hear yourself think?
U niqueness is fun,
E ven though it's just you, just think there's no one else like you.

Emily Tritton (11)
Maidenhill School, Stonehouse

MY DOG COOKIE

My dog stares up at me
Her eyes are open wide
Her little tail wagging
And her head tilted one side.
She seeks my attention
As she'd missed me all day long
I've missed her too, oh so much
We really get along.
She really is the best dog
I've really ever had
And I try and make the most
Of the special times we've had.
I really love my special friend
She's cuddly and so warm
I love to sit her on my lap
And pat her while she snores.
There will come a day
Where she's no longer with me
But we'll remember all the times
We had together dearly.

Cloe Griffiths (11)
Maidenhill School, Stonehouse

WEMBLEY

The biggest, the best . . . Wembley!
90,000 seats, two changing rooms and one pitch
Most of the best have played there
Most of the best have made history there
The place where fans chant on and on
The place where players dream to play
Like bees and honey, drawing fans in one by one
The place where dreams are achieved
And where dreams are shattered.
The best . . . Wembley!

Joe Davis (12)
Maidenhill School, Stonehouse

THE FIVE SENSES OF HAPPINESS

The wonderful smell of bacon.
The smell of the beautiful forest.
The amazing smell of the light blue sea.
The mouth-watering smell and taste of waffles.
The delicious taste of Friday's sweet day.
The taste of Winstones ice cream is like heaven.
The taste of the finest bubblegum milkshake.
The sound of the bell at the end of the day.
The peaceful sound of the open fire crackling.
The great sound of music.
The contagious sound of laughter.
The touch of my furry guinea pig.
The comfort of my warm bed.
The touch of the football at my feet.
The warmth of hugs.
The sight of my uncles at the front door.
The outstanding sight from my bedroom window.
The sight of my family.
The sight of my scrumptious tea.

Rudi Churchill (11)
Maidenhill School, Stonehouse

POPPIES

The poppy of life
The poppy of love
The poppy for remembering
The power of the poppy is to repair a broken soul
A single poppy can be cherished in a heart
Kindness to others
And true thanks to strangers
They will fight all day for victory
For me, for you, for us, for everyone
We will remember them
Today and always.

Mikayla Bingle (12)
Maidenhill School, Stonehouse

ALONE

I am a fading shadow,
Like a blur.
No one hears me,
No one understands
Just who I really am.
Every night I dread to think
Of what tomorrow's going to bring.
Anger, fury, rage, frustration.
I sit and wonder what's life's worth living for.
Fun, happiness, cheering, joy and excitement.
Why hasn't that come to me?
Why can't the world cooperate?
Sad, unhappy, I wonder why.
Why am I a shadow,
Never seeming to appear?
I'm not clear to anyone,
I'm a blur, sad, my life is just loneliness.
I'm all . . .
Alone.

Abbie Cathryn Allen (12)
Maidenhill School, Stonehouse

DREAMS AND WISHES

Hope to others around you,
Give faith to everyone,
Believe in yourself,
Good luck, you will need it,
An angel is always by your side,
Wishes can come true,
Dream to make life better,
There can be good vs bad,
Anything can have dreams and wishes,
Including you!

Maizy Gregory (11)
Maidenhill School, Stonehouse

TEENAGE DRAMA

Being a teenager can be a very hard time,
You go through heartbreak, gossip and worse
But sometimes you don't know when to pull the line,
However, you may pull the line when it comes to losers!

But come on, don't let any boy trouble
Get in your way beautiful girl.
Just get your favourite teddy and give it a cuddle,
Now shake your mind and give it a twirl.

'Oh no, 1 . . . 2 . . . 3 teenage spots!'
Just give them a little touch of cream,
So they will shrink and look like little dots,
They won't be as bad as what you dream!

Now it's time to prepare to become an adult,
By being responsible, sensible about what you do,
So don't act like a cute little pup,
Woah, what a lot of things a teenager goes through!

Chelsey Kelly Mauler (12)
Maidenhill School, Stonehouse

HORSE RIDING

H orse jumping, jump by jump!
O ver and over again
R osettes being won, every competition
S addles being put on a horse for another ride
E very horse has a rest so they can gain some more energy

R ides and rides happening again and again
I watch the horses roll in the field
D ancing all around
I sit there and watch and wonder what it's like to be a pony
N o other noises apart from horses and ponies neighing
G etting rest and sleep after a long day at work because tomorrow is going to be another amazing day.

Faith Bonsor (11)
Maidenhill School, Stonehouse

HEARTBREAKER

You think he's perfect,
You think he's Mr Right,
You think you'll win his heart
And you won't have to fight.
You think you'll stay together
Through day and through night.

Then he starts ignoring you,
He starts talking to other girls,
Calling them pretty,
Running his fingers through their curls,
He tells them he loves them in front of your face,
He tells you to die because he thinks you're a disgrace.

Then you get a text,
Saying you're done,
Your heart has broken,
The good times – gone.

Bonnie Denning (11)
Maidenhill School, Stonehouse

THE LAKE

I am sat by the lake,
watching the whistling wind
ruffle my hair.

As I stood I could hear
the tinkling of the ice cream van
as all the children run out of school.

My senses flip as I smell
the lucky child's dinner
of fish and chips.

I bend down and feel
the roughness of the leaves
beneath my feet.

Grace Knight (12)
Maidenhill School, Stonehouse

WHEN I'M A TEENAGER ...

Being a teenager must be hard because there's so many questions
that I just have to ask!

Will I have an abrupt and uncountable change of mood every hour?

Every time I see my parents after school
will I have an instantaneous argument or an emotional fallout?

Will I change my school rucksack to a designer handbag?

Do I wear my clear, natural lip gloss
or change to a cherry-red, luminous, thick lipstick?

Shall I wear my vibrant, vivid trainers
or swap them for a pair of stylish, shiny daps with a heel?

Is there more melodramatic friend drama to appear?

Do all these changes have to be made
or do I stick to my normal ways?

Eve Phillips (11)
Maidenhill School, Stonehouse

THE FUTURE, 5099

My father connected controls to the pod
As I jumped out of my warm hoverbed.

Calling my name. '9617,' he said with a nod,
'Hurry up, the overlord has issued a command.'

'All pods move to the destination
And connect yourselves to the jugger pad.'

We notified the overlord of our location.

'Load your supplies of food and weapons,
We are going on an expedition.'

We swallowed the food in tablet form
And away we sped . . .
To the black hole and unknown fate.

Maxson Thomas (11)
Maidenhill School, Stonehouse

LOOKING INTO THE FUTURE

When I look into the future
There are flying cars
People on Mars
Sugarless chocolate bars
But there aren't any stars.

When I look into the future
There are people flying around with jet packs
Big fat rats that eat cats
Poisonous bats
But there aren't any cafes to eat at.

When I look into the future
The sky is purple
The paths are made of marble
There's spaceships in the harbour
But there aren't any barbers.

Connor Durrant (12)
Maidenhill School, Stonehouse

MY HOLIDAY

My holiday was the best
Turquoise sea, sparkling waves
Paddling, jumping, then ice-cold splashes
Golden sand, rough underfoot
Chestnut horse trotting proudly along
Narrow gauge engines chuffing merrily
Steam lingering in the moorland sky
A rainy day. Hooray for soft play!
Great excitement, my brother's arms flapping wildly
As he throws himself down the slide
A welcoming lick from an old friend
Pets corner is a happy place to be
Time to go home, sad to leave
My holiday was the best.

Patrick Holland (11)
Maidenhill School, Stonehouse

GRAMP

Gramp, I know you're gone,
But I will never forget,
The times we had sat on your bed.
You gave me advice,
On lots of life.
I always knew I could come to you!

Each night I look up at the sky,
To see you are there.
The brightest shining star in the sky,
Staring down at me with a loving glare.

You made me laugh,
You made me smile,
You also made me sad for a while,
But now I know you will never be far away,
I just can't see you!

Tyler Needham (11)
Maidenhill School, Stonehouse

CHILD AND TEENAGER DREAM

Everyone tells you
They are the best years of your life,
From a child to a teenager,
In less than a year.

As a child you are free,
As a teenager you feel tied up,
A child has no worries,
A teenager has lots.

I am looking in a mirror,
But all I see is me,
Trying to be
What I want to be,
Instead of what I really am.

Paris Rogers (11)
Maidenhill School, Stonehouse

FRIENDS

Until the end, they are your friends.

F riends are
R emembered
I n your hearts
E ven when nobody
N otices them or you
D on't disappoint, for they are
S pecial

F or you shall not forget
O r ever let them down
R emember the good times when
E veryone thought you were different
V ictory, triumph as you prove them wrong
E veryone recognises them
R emember your friends until the end.

Bella Hannis (11)
Maidenhill School, Stonehouse

THE SURFER

The thrill, the rush, it feels like I'm flying.
The glistening water, the white sandy beach
As the sun sets on the white horses
I flow through the stalking waves.
The board cutting up the wave like a hot knife through butter,
Viciously turning left and right
As a race to the seashore begins.
The danger, the unknown, what's under the surface?
Mermaids? Sharks? Or the unexpected jellyfish?
As I meander through the crashing waves. *Splash!*
Lost in the abyss,
Tumble after tumble, roll after roll.
Where am I?

Archie Curtis (12)
Maidenhill School, Stonehouse

XBOX

Xbox, Xbox is my life,
Xbox, Xbox toil and strife.
It's not a game, it's real life.
I even play until midnight.
If I had it my way
I would play all night.
That's just me and I'm loving life.

I play with my controller and my friends,
We use our headsets to connect, talk and make amends.
The games we play are not friendly or sweet,
It's violence. We fight till one's left standing!
When my batteries are drained all out
I'll run downstairs and get more out
But if there's none left I just get stressy,
Go watch 'Friends' on telly and wait till tea's ready.

Isaac Wathern (11)
Maidenhill School, Stonehouse

IN THE FUTURE

In the future, what will the world come to?
Will robots rule our lives, in the future?
Or will they bring happiness, in the future?
Will technology manipulate our minds, in the future?
Or will it work for us, in the future?
Will we sleep in fear, in the future?
Or will we sing in happiness, in the future?
Will our world be a toxic wasteland, in the future?
Or will it be luscious and green, in the future?
Will we be bored of hovering, in the future?
Or will we ride hoverboards in pride, in the future?
Will we live in poverty, in the future?
Or will we be rich and popular, in the future?

I'm looking forward to my future!

Ollie Thomson (11)
Maidenhill School, Stonehouse

LOOK UP

Look up, look up,
Stop hiding your outside life!
There's a life out there,
Not just on a screen.

There are more things to do,
You have a life,
Live it to the fullest,
Just remember if you want to succeed
You have to believe!

Remember there will be hard times,
And if you make the effort
You will succeed.

If you find it hard looking up,
Look up and don't look down.

Harvey Long (11)
Maidenhill School, Stonehouse

OUR FUTURE

Our future can change the world.
Day and night flying cars go by.
Kids speeding to school on hoverboards.
Teleporters sending you to the moon and back.
Houses with talking fridges and intelligent cookers
Saving you time and energy.
Cakes talking to you, saying, 'You've eaten too much.'
If only time now could be like this.

Our future can destroy the world.
Robots taking over our minds,
Making us think we are one of them.
Computers taking over, leaving viruses at every turn.
What will this world evolve into?
Only we can stop the future destroying our world.

Harry Baxter (12)
Maidenhill School, Stonehouse

MR UNICORN

O Mr Unicorn, O Mr Unicorn,
Seems quite lonely,
Looks to the sky but no one's
There to play with.

O Mr Unicorn, O Mr Unicorn,
Goes adventuring,
Finds a cave that's quite gloomy!
What happens next? he thought.

O Mr Unicorn, O Mr Unicorn,
Goes into the cave, lights appear!
'Hip hip hooray, he's here!'
Said some other unicorns.

O Mr Unicorn, O Mr Unicorn,
Is no longer lonely . . .

Callum Cheeseman (11)
Maidenhill School, Stonehouse

ISLAND

The dark green trees sway side to side,
As the breeze makes the light leaves
Like feathers flying off into the warm, bright blue sea.
As it slowly moves towards the soft warm sand,
Gently swaying across the tall, spiky pineapple.
As it rolls into the bright, sunny and green distance
Tall green trees sway in front of the colourful birds,
Singing sweet songs as the beach house shines,
Beautiful and lovely in the fading out background.
The sweet and sour lemons fall from the green trees
As the bluebirds dance towards the sun.
This is paradise.

Isabel Workman (11)
Maidenhill School, Stonehouse

UNTITLED

The start of the new year, wow!
How the time has flown,
As I leave the past behind me from a brilliant year,
This time of the year is for parties and celebrating.
What a good time we had last year with friends and family,
As we look to the future,
We will work hard,
We will help others,
We will be fair and we will support other people.
This year I'm going to improve my skills in school,
Especially in geography
Because I need a better grade.
I'm looking forward to all the sport competitions.
I wish you a happy new year and the best of luck
To help you achieve your goals and dreams.

Sammy Counter (11)
Maidenhill School, Stonehouse

THE ROLLER COASTER

The queue is long and winds right round
To where the roller coaster can be found.
The buzz is loud as people talk.
You can hear people scream like a hawk.
The roaring of the track above,
We are nearly there as we hear a shout,
'Hold on tight and don't fall out!'
We are here at last, I think it's going to be a blast,
I hold on tight and off we go, up, up,
Up we climb because it's roller coaster time.
Whoosh! Off we go, upside down, inside out,
Round and round, my tummy just fell out!
All of a sudden we come to a stop,
Off we get and our legs are like jelly,
We walk to the end to see ourselves on the telly!

Charlie Parkes (11)
Maidenhill School, Stonehouse

MY DREAM FOR THE FUTURE

I want to be a teacher
Being loving and caring to them
To help encourage them
Push them to their limits
Put a smile on their faces when sad
Putting a frown upside down makes my day
Even if it's a hey
And if it puts a smile on their face
That makes me happy and joyful inside.
Looking after children,
Seeing them having fun,
Learning and having fun, that's my goal.

Molly Walker (11)
Maidenhill School, Stonehouse

NIGHTMARE

In the creaky, spooky woods
A boy was wandering,
A scream . . .

And then he turned,
A tree screaming,
Sap dripping like blood,
A scary wood,
A man hacking away at the tree.

Then he turned and glared.
He ran rapidly at the boy . . .
He shrieks in terror as he wakes up.

Nathaniel Thornton (11)
Maidenhill School, Stonehouse

CYCLING

Here are a few reasons why I love cycling . . .

C arrying on no matter what
Y ou get to places quicker
C ycling no matter who's judging you
L oving the freedom
I 'm encouraging other people to start cycling
N ever giving up
G oing everywhere – no matter what

That's why in a world of pain and grief
Cycling is my escape, my life!
I love cycling and no one can take that away from me!

Keavey Willis (12)
Maidenhill School, Stonehouse

IPAD

I love my iPad
For every day
There's some new game to play.

There are many apps on my iPad to see
Like movies, games just for me.
It's good to have to watch
And play on a rainy day.
The battery doesn't last very long,
Off you go to charge it up.
When it says 100% it's ready to go
So my iPad, it's great to play and go.

Adam David Pope (12)
Maidenhill School, Stonehouse

CLUB BOWLING 300 GAME

Ball in the gutter, red and blue shoes,
So happy to get a strike,
Seeing flashing lights too!

Entertainment at Stroud,
Positioning the right angle to get a high score,
Then suddenly to be defeated by the girls.

Excited to play an enjoyable game,
Deflated when shooting a 4-6 split in my lane.

Bowling's a game I love most of all,
The *bang!* and the *clatter!* of the pins as they fall.

Simon Bermingham (11)
Maidenhill School, Stonehouse

PARIS-ROUBAIX

Riding down cobbled roads of death.
The taste of blood in my chest.
One more bend until the end.

The finish line in sight,
I pedalled with all my might.

The hours I sacrificed for this one race,
A medal will put a smile on my face.

Paris-Roubaix, what a race!

Stanley Shilton (12)
Maidenhill School, Stonehouse

PHEASANT PIE

I'm never happier than when I'm out in the field.
With my gun in my hand and my dog at my heel.

The sound of the birds flying high.
My shotgun pointing towards the blue sky.

The beaters are out and the birds are in flight.
If we want supper, this has to be right.

I pulled my trigger and I heard the bird cry.
My dog went running, yes, that's pheasant pie!

Barnaby Moore (11)
Maidenhill School, Stonehouse

I LOVE SKATING

It's such a blast, I go so fast,
Around the hall, you will fall,
Have a laugh, with the staff,
Skate for three hours, having a million powers,
With your mates, on your skates,
You will learn, when it comes to your turn,
For the limbo you skate slow
And bend down low.
So this is my skating poem.

Sky Thomas (12)
Maidenhill School, Stonehouse

FOOD AND DRINK

Food and drink is something you swallow
Even if your throat is hollow.
Pizza is in triangles not like Pringles.
Coke isn't something to poke.
Chips are what you dunk into dips.
Fanta is a fruit banta.
Pasta is what Rasta eats.
Lasagne isn't made from Ghana.
When you digest don't you think you should suggest!

Bayley Thomas Knight (12)
Maidenhill School, Stonehouse

THE WIND

The wind blowing through my hair
Like a fresh summer breeze.
The wind blowing through my body
Like a ghostly presence.
The wind stopping to get some air
From all that blowing.
The weird, majestic wind,
Show me your face,
Show me your best blow.

Charlie Green (11)
Maidenhill School, Stonehouse

CHOCOLATE

Chocolate, chocolate, chocolate,
A birthday cake my dad would make.
Chocolate, chocolate, chocolate,
We covered it in Smarties, buttons and a Flake.
Chocolate, chocolate, chocolate,
A birthday treat it was.
Chocolate, chocolate, chocolate,
Burning bright were candles and a little tune was sang.
I blew out the candles and the chocolate feast began.

Charlie Thomas Rudge (11)
Maidenhill School, Stonehouse

CARS FROM THE FUTURE

Flying cars are great
Hovering every day.
They're super fast but being defeated by the girls.
At the car park, in the air
Everyone's scared so they lose their hair.
Then the car parks turn it into a hover bike and scooter park.
It's too loud so the dogs bark.
Cars are what I like the most.
My favourite car is a Ferrari.

Cameron James Bishop (12)
Maidenhill School, Stonehouse

SPIDERS

S pooky spiders make me screech
P rickly legs and ugly teeth
I nto the web I shall be!
D ie! Die! Die!
E xterminate that disturbing thing
R un away! Leave me be!
S pooky spiders, now I'll be free.

Cristian Rieger (11)
Maidenhill School, Stonehouse

A LIFE AS A LION

The lion ducks down like a ninja,
Completely unseen.
He pounces on his prey.
After he kills his prey he runs back to his pride.
The cubs eat the kill.
After they eat they sleep with their mum.
I go outside to weep and then I sleep.
The next day the lioness tells me to take cover.
As she goes off to hunt I think that life's hard.

Samuel Coombs (11)
Maidenhill School, Stonehouse

I HAVE FLOATED AWAY

I have floated away,
To a place so far away,
Floated so far away,
That no one could ever find me again.

Yet I do not know the feeling of weightlessness,
Because I cannot break away from the deceptive weight of the world,
Impelling me to the ground,
But it's met with a feeling of my insides being heaved out through my lips
And forced back down again.

And the flowers that grow inside of my chest are being yanked out maliciously,
By a mind-killing monster who destroys them for no reason at all,
But I'd like to thank him actually,
For giving me the artistry to create a perfect place filled with solitude,
Which could be a good thing and a bad thing really.

And my heart, I've discovered is a heart of lead,
With painful palpitations,
Meagre motivations,
Imperilled infactuations.

And my brain is battering against the walls of my skull,
So violently that I start to feel colour
And through my chaotic mind
I can feel the coldness of black touching me.

And I fear that I have floated away,
That I have floated so far away,
That no one could ever find me again,
Not even me.

Abhirami Santhosh-Pillai (16)
Methodist College, Belfast

I DON'T WRITE POETRY BECAUSE . . .

I don't write poetry because
The words, orchestral in my head, seem restricted on a page.
They drip instead of flow onto paper.

It's not like they don't make sense,
But rather they don't want to.
Rebellious against the formality of poetry.

The sentences won't run like smooth coherent lines,
That hint at something deeper
Than words uniform like soldiers on a page.

The words sit flat and angry and bruised.
They don't run and jump and laugh and hop
Or dance and sing and rhyme and pop.

They just tumble out as a mess on the page.
A riot of bad spelling amongst illegible writing.
They taunt like jagged threads of flowing lines,
Angry that they are stuck to the paper by ink.

Poetry is for the sophisticated.
The wise and knowing who drink red wine
And read 'The Guardian' with a frown.

It's full of unattainable words
And metaphors I will never get.
An underlying theme I couldn't see
A visual everyone got but me.

So because is why I don't write
Poetry.

Lydia Franklin (16)
Methodist College, Belfast

A BOY PENNED FROM A PAGE

A voice full of passion
His posture tall and proud,
His feet did not seem to tread upon the ground.

His eyes honey-hazel
With thick glasses were trimmed,
His complexion, his pallor the sun had not dimmed.

He questioned their teachings
With his ideals and mirth,
And had answers to questions put to him since birth.

He was haloed by curls
Which caressed his head,
Unlike his, my own, which hung lifeless and dead.

We met at the library,
But how did this start?
I fell in love with his logic, his humour, his heart.

I was a girl
Brought to life by the page,
Tired of living a life as though acting on stage.

He had to return,
Brought to life from the page
Paper cuts and nicks, that's all I could save.

But out of our shipwreck,
There's a lesson to learn.
That those who shine brightest have touches that burn.

Sofina Ali (16)
Methodist College, Belfast

IF I COULD GO BACK

If I could go back
I would say to mankind:
Cherish your planet,
You've got only one.

If I could go back
I would say to the state:
Keep brawling for sway,
Who cares about life?

If I could go back
I would say to the public:
Do not thrash the plants,
You'll weep for their life.

If I could go back
I would tell humankind:
Exult nature's colours,
They'll soon burn in air.

If I could go back
I would say to myself:
Do something about it,
It'll go a long way.

Now from afar
To my planet I say,
'I'm sorry . . . it's late.'

César Fernández Llamera (16)
Methodist College, Belfast

THEY'RE DIFFERENT (THE SAME)

She closed her eyes, counted to ten,
bit back her words and played pretend.
He told himself, 'Just one more day,
one more day 'til I go far away.'
She held in a flood behind those eyes,
too smart to talk, she stayed in disguise.
He tried to leave but couldn't go far. No.
Not with this little sister at home; his dad in the bar.

She suffered through school, through social hell,
sat behind him in maths and couldn't tell,
that this was his escape from a volatile home,
'cause he was surrounded by friends, she was alone.
They collided in the corridor and she let out a squeak
because he was popular and she was a 'freak'.
What's her problem? he thought to himself.
Well, she'd rather be at home with her nose in the bookshelf.

They parted ways without a glance.
Their paths had crossed just by chance.
As his day got better, hers got worse
and when school was over, this hit reverse.
He prayed to his mum, *let my sister be alright*
'cause his dad hits girls. His dad's not nice.
But she finally felt safe and took off her mask,
kicked off her shoes and just relaxed.

Katie Gillespie (16)
Methodist College, Belfast

TONGUE UNTIED

My unarticulated tongue
wraps around words unformed
and blistering to be spilled
from my bruised mouth.

My hands numb
from the touch they never felt,
grown tired of emptiness
they flop lifeless.

My mutilated heart
chipped and chopped,
each time, every time
lest I forgot . . .

My dead body
cradled by a box,
crushed from the earth
deep down below.

The words will forever
puncture my throat,
cut my mind,
Scar my soul.

Ceara Harper (16)
Methodist College, Belfast

SILENT BUT SUBJECT

Beads of water travel elegantly,
keeping fast and faultless all the while.
Their landing causes subtle chaos
and she can paint a smile.

We are quick to admire the gracefulness;
something is fitting about their fall.
Any mess made can be wiped away;
she is silent but subject to it all.

Wipe clean the debris of the droplet,
overlook it, pretend it wasn't there.
Stick around for the easy beforehand
and she will never feel that you care.

What seems easy is easy to engage in
and what seems intense might make you want to run.
But don't let your insecurities haunt you
and don't let your friendships come undone.

We all need somebody to talk to,
a good friend more often than not.
Watch a teardrop fall in slow motion,
watch it crash and give it a thought.

Zara Aylward-Maruna (16)
Methodist College, Belfast

KITE POEM

I made a small kite
it was prepped for flight
an elongated square
it was quite bare
but it did not matter
for the sky it could flatter.

I ran against the breeze
it came up with ease
the clouds it would pierce
ever so fierce
the birds it could match
comets it could catch
the planes it could race
almost touching space
it was the king of sky
higher than the high.

I let go of the string
to let it be king
of the big blue sky
highest of the high.

Luka Fuchs (14)
Methodist College, Belfast

THE BEGGAR GIRL

The rain pours down and there's loud noises outside
Horns beep, engines sound and little birds hide.
A little lonely figure standing in the rain,
Hands cupped, arms outstretched, kneeling there in vain.
The poor soul sitting there soaked from head to toe,
Clothes ripped, shoes worn and the harsh winds blow.
Her ragged little face looking down at the ground,
But everyone could see how she frowned.
Cars rustled past, not aware of her existence,
Some people just looked, from a distance.
Not a single penny in her frozen, blue hands
At the side of a street, a little girl stands.
Not a single, kind person took pity;
Not a single human being in the city.
The heartless creatures rushed past her
Brushing her with their warm coats of fur.
How she really wished she had a bed to sleep.
Frozen, she buried her head in her chest
And water dripped out of her delicate little eyes;
Tears.

Yifei Shen (11)
Methodist College, Belfast

LITTLE RED

As I stand on the deserted moors
Blood-red cape fluttering in the wind
I stand contemplating my life
In the Land of Fairy Tales
Where happily ever afters are beginning and ending
Every second dreams are coming true.
But then I realise
I never got a happily ever after.
Sure, I escaped a near-death experience
Yet I can't help but feel jealous of the others
With their princes and fine clothes and wealth.
All I got was being cut out of the stupid wolf's stomach.
But in the end,
Life is just waiting for your wolf to pounce.

Niamh O'Connor (12)
Methodist College, Belfast

IMMORTAL

You rise,
Not yet at your apex,
The low lights of the sky glow turquoise,
As you shine with your comforting yet distant light,
You are not either but both the sun and the moon,
Everlasting yet untouchable,
Truly immortal.

Tashfia Ahmed (13)
Methodist College, Belfast

HANSEL AND GRETEL

When you think of a nursery rhyme
You think of a tale that's as old as time
And so my dears, the story starts
A different version, but don't take it to heart
A story of two frightful youths
And how they met the witch with a big sweet tooth.

To Hansel and Gretel their parents said one day,
'You awful kids, please go away,
We cannot take your frightful way,
So go out to the woods please we pray.'
And off they went so bad and bold,
Unaware of the house the colour of gold.

Soon they came to a glade and there
They found a house they just couldn't bear!
'Oh joy, oh glory, see what we spied,
A house made of sweets!' they happily cried.
The house was indeed an entire feast,
And still not aware that owner was a beast.

The door flew open and standing there
Was a wonderful lady that would help and care.
'Come a little closer dears, let me have a look,'
And she threw them into her oven and left them there to cook.
This is where the story ends, I know a very sudden crunch
But please remember to be nice or get eaten up for lunch.

Olivia Edwards-Cox (13)
Millais School, Horsham

SOLDIER BOY

He marches on
Surrounded by fellow soldiers.

He marches on
Gun in hand.

He marches on
What is he going to do?

This is it
It's time.

This is war!

Rebecca Childs (12)
Millais School, Horsham

NATURE'S MONOLOGUE

One must avenge with vengeance
The wrongs must be undone
The wrath of nature they must face
To put humans back in their place.

A waste of water
Must be punished by drought
They took advantage of what they had
They now must go without.

A majestic bird flies on the wind
Through skies too great to measure
That same great bird plummets to the ground
For humanity's sickest pleasure.

They underestimate my power
Their steps they must retrace
Or I will shake the Earth
And they'll tremble in their place.

Until humanity respects the Earth
Their home that they must cherish
Nature will avenge with vengeance
So the Earth will never perish.

Ella McIntosh & Maya Espinet
Notre Dame School, Cobham

UNTITLED

A poem is a group of words
A song with no lyrics
Lyrics with no song
It's a rhythm with no blues
Poems are our muse.

A poem we have to learn
To find the art of the world
They're the songs we sing and hear
Without a whisper of a great peer.

They are written by seeing the beauty
Of sights, smell and well
Just about anything
We learn them in school
Not as punishment
To find the deepest meaning of someone who was deeply out of it
But to hear a story in minutes flat
To change a life in a moment
So quick even a song couldn't do.

So I say when you hear your next poem
Of a collection of words
Don't worry about the teacher
Telling you the meaning
It's a story for you
To interpret how you please
Please don't think it's a punishment to seize
It's a moment that might change you
For better or for worse
But it's a moment none the better
So take it in your verse.

Imogen Bendall
Notre Dame School, Cobham

AFTERMATH

The sand skims along the earth's dry crevices.
The last of some cattle, that were left behind
are enveloped, lovingly, by the flies -
eviscerated,
their fur drapes over their pale bones like crumpled silk.

In the breeze, the dust and sand
interweaves through the thatched huts,
lonely and crumbling.
And the deadly pattern of the cracked bronze earth
crawls up their walls now,
and threatens to dismantle them.

Now – the sun burns more brightly
than the roofs had done.
And the air's quietude, cries,
louder . . . even louder
than the children did,
and it's none the more beautiful.

Within the stillness, the sand and the ash
still circling,
hushes their distressed echoes,
but the breeze breathes it back on its way.
And the place resumes its silence, after its passing.

Amy Anne Claire Berton (16)
Notre Dame School, Cobham

UTOPIAN DYSTOPIA

White walls surround me.
I can't breathe.
I can't see.
The walls are closing in.
Help me.

Black:
Pitch-black.
I can hear voices
Footsteps coming towards me.
Help me.
I don't know where I am.

It's beautiful
The green landscapes
The bright blue sky
The soft grass crumples
Beneath my feet
The sun warms my skin.

The soft waves
Crash at my feet
Birds singing
In the treetops
It's all so perfect: Utopia.

The stars shine so bright
In the darkness,
They look so close
Yet so far away,
I try to reach them
But I'm trapped

Here
Forever.

Emma Rostron (14)
Salendine Nook High School, Huddersfield

LITTLE BOX

I wish I had a little box,
With hinges made of gold
And that when I held it
In my hand,
It could warm away the cold.

It would be
Small enough,
To fit inside my heart,
So when the frost grew too deep,
It would melt the frost apart.

The power of my little box
With special treasure hid,
Would be that when a tear fell,
Could open up its lid.

Inside would be the sweet fresh air,
Of a shimmering summer's day,
With flowers of spring, autumn leaves
And a cool splash of sea spray.

And a hug
To keep me warm and feeling safe at night.
So when the woe and dark descend
There are no tears
In sight.

Zainab Khalid (14)
Salendine Nook High School, Huddersfield

RUNNING FOR UTOPIA

A wave of air flies past,
Running, leaping, bounding away,
Snow falling on the yellow grass,
The hunt starts today.

They carry weapons,
Purposely for striking us down,
Our rare fur is their desire
And to take us to the ground.

Now. They're coming,
I can hear their horses.
The clatter of guns,
Their loud voices.

A chase for freedom,
To avoid defeat.
Whipping against their faces
The wind they must beat.

They have no direction,
They just want a paradise,
A place they can call home.
Where they don't have to fight,
The hunt ends tomorrow.

Molly Nicholson (13)
Salendine Nook High School, Huddersfield

TIMES AND TECH

The past; what isn't left to see.
Old wagons, no cars with technology
Going on into big flashes and the two-seated motor
Next, big phones that shrink to the size of a protractor
Bulky televisions with a black and white motion picture
And big computers with the new worldwide web; a large mixture,
They all *seemed* amazing . . .

The present; the time is now, not before.
Touch screen laptops and big phones once more
Compact cameras and cars that race at 270 miles an hour
High definition and three-dimensional cinema to devour
Popular music and auditory speakers with earphones
And TVs less than a centimetre thick with many clones,
They all *seem* amazing . . .

The future; what is yet to find us at our core.
High-speed hovercrafts outside every door
Televisions turning into holograms, leaping all around you
Living amongst artificial human beings and animals, no curfew
Microchips inside our eyes to capture an image of what we do
And maybe even meet an extraterrestrial man or two,
These all *are* amazing.

Hannah Ayesha Ghulam (11)
Salendine Nook High School, Huddersfield

THE WASTELAND

What was once the world,
Now, a fetid lump.
What was once a great country,
Now ruled by Trump.
When the bombs fell, nothing was right.
What were once simple creatures now fill us with fright.
The Statue of Liberty, blown away in a gust,
New York City: nothing but dust.
Nothing is alive, nothing is here.
Even the voices that drift in my ears.
Those who were once mechanical protectors:
Now vicious brutes, now defectors.
I lie in the dark, filled with fright.
What was once sweet happiness now is plight.
The radiation seeps in, slow, like a fleet.
Hell, I have eyes on my feet!

I stand in the ruins, drenched in mud.
The things around here thirst for blood.
The future – no hovercrafts, just a shell.
We made it out to be Heaven, but it turned into Hell.

Daniel Knott (12)
Salendine Nook High School, Huddersfield

SPACE

Have you ever thought of the mysteries of our night sky?
Children always wonder why.
Scientists think they know everything about our solar system . . . they do not.
Have you heard of the black hole?
It is a foe,
The sun is the hottest star,
It can melt a car.
We live in the Milky Way.
Other galaxies they lay.
On Earth people watch the comet shower,
It is as high as the tallest tower.
Have you had a look at Mars?
On Earth it is as big as all the cars
And all the other planets in our galaxy,
Sadly you won't be able to get a chocolate galaxy.
Mesmerising is our solar system.

Soha Khaliq (11)
Salendine Nook High School, Huddersfield

ENERGY

A myriad of wires and metal,
Clanking down the Cinder Block Avenue,
Rusted metal littering the streets.
A lone figure stood desolate upon,
A mountain of scrap.

Creaking joints and clanking feet,
Crawling towards the flickering clump of twisted metal.
A power line, a pylon,
Crushed by the wars.

The clanking stopped as its joints seized,
Metal crumpling as it fell,
Down to the Cinder Block Street.
The flickering light dimmed,
Before finally going out,
Forever dim, forever dark.

Nova Smith (14)
Salendine Nook High School, Huddersfield

RIP – WHO WAS HE?

Resting where?
In Heaven or Hell?
Preventing what, happiness?

Why did he commit suicide?
How did he commit suicide?
Only because of me?

What happens now he is gone?
All will change, even me!
Scares me, these thoughts they are my fear.

How will this end?
Exactly, is this what you wanted?
Evie, a daughter without a father.

Libby Kaye Ackroyd (12)
Salendine Nook High School, Huddersfield

WHAT COMES NEXT?

Hear the footsteps getting closer and closer,
Shadows looming round every door.
The black spider becomes real,
Clasping my neck tight fast,
What to do, can't do anything,
What have I done?
They've already won,
Ready for the blue stripes,
The end of a life.

Orwell has warned us about constant surveillance,
Atwood warns us of the effect of a nuclear war,
Collins considered humans as sports.

Is this truly what humans are capable of?
What could throw us next?

Esther Barrett (13)
Salendine Nook High School, Huddersfield

I LOVE HIM

Shiny, black coals, lined with mascara,
gazing up at me,
his face radiant with light,
dirty nose and sooty paws,
white tail and a tan body covered in fluffy feathers,
hovering by the doorway,
silently, waiting to be admonished,
but I could not resist his loving look,
as he twisted his body and licked my hand . . .
his tail rising in waiting hope,
for me to come home!
Once again he is my loyal companion,
therefore we will always be friends!

Lark Gneiting (11)
The Christian School, Bishop's Stortford

FIDDLY THING

I like to fiddle with my fiddly thing
It's fuzzy and hard and soft.
I bend it the way I want to
But one day it got lost.

My friend Josh took it
He told me a while after.
When he told me it was a prank
He was filled with laughter.

Sometimes I stick a pencil through it
And spin it round and round.
I watch the spirals do their thing
But sometimes it falls off to the ground.

It twists across my fingers
Exactly like a snake.
And if I want to make it different
Sometimes I make it break.

Aaron Walker (12)
The Christian School, Bishop's Stortford

IT'S 2033, I ALMOST FORGOT THAT TOO!

Machines can help people in desperate need too.
Continents can be friends, everyone too.
Monkeys can fly on geothermal jet packs, dogs too.
Want to be prime minister? That interests me too.
Violence is banned in England, Donald T too (phew)!
Littering is illegal, making life safer too.
Hovercrafts are invented, making travel easy to the zoo.
The war is over, taxes too (I wish).
. . . It is 2033, almost forgot that too!

Joshua O Williams (11)
The Christian School, Bishop's Stortford

STOP THE APOCALYPSE SQUAD!

The year is 3550 AD, when humans live on Jupiter,
and peace could never be worse
because now the Apocalypse Squad has risen
and has said Jupiter is a curse.
They stopped the peace and started war,
the battle was very tense.
The Apocalypse Squad won, and slaughtered our soldiers,
it really didn't make sense.
That some would do such a thing,
they were very evil indeed;
so we must send out our armies,
in our serious time in need.
Because it is Jupiter's end as we know it,
we can't let it go on;
we must stop the Apocalypse Squad,
or our world will be gone.

Ben De Vos (11)
The Christian School, Bishop's Stortford

MY PUPPY

She is a cute little furball that likes a sprint,
A quiet panting girl who really needs a mint.
She is a cheeky adventurer and is easily intrigued,
If she digs up the garden beds my mum will gather fury,
A small, silky, white back with little hazel ears,
When she licks all the glass she leaves big smears,
She sleeps and she plays, like any normal pup,
Quite crazy all the time, like when she drank in a cup,
I cherish my pup so much, she's treasured like a gem,
A new part of my family, even if she causes mayhem.

Eleanor Grace Chichlowska (12)
The Christian School, Bishop's Stortford

MY PHONE

'No,' answered my mother.
'Why?' I replied as I sighed.
'I said no.'
'Why can't I have a phone? All my friends do.'
My mother is always doing this.
I'm eleven and all I want is a phone.
She can be so mean sometimes.
She'll say, 'Oh, please don't moan.'
I write stories, books, films and more.
Then, it happened as I saw her walk in the door.
'Here,' she said.
'Here, I have it, an amazing phone right here in its pocket.
Be gentle, be oh so gentle, cos it's very dear to me for eternity.
What's wrong? Is that so extraordinary, odd, bizarre, weird?'
She said with great fear.
'No, I'm happy, I'm oh so happy. I can't wait to tell Saffy.'

Milly O'Connor (11)
The Christian School, Bishop's Stortford

YoungWriters
Est. 1991

YOUNG WRITERS INFORMATION

We hope you have enjoyed reading this book – and that you will continue to in the coming years.

If you're a young writer who enjoys reading and creative writing, or the parent of an enthusiastic poet or story writer, do visit our website www.youngwriters.co.uk. Here you will find free competitions, workshops and games, as well as recommended reads, a poetry glossary and our blog.

If you would like to order further copies of this book, or any of our other titles give us a call or visit **www.youngwriters.co.uk**.

Young Writers
Remus House
Coltsfoot Drive
Peterborough
PE2 9BF

(01733) 890066
info@youngwriters.co.uk